THE UNITED STATES

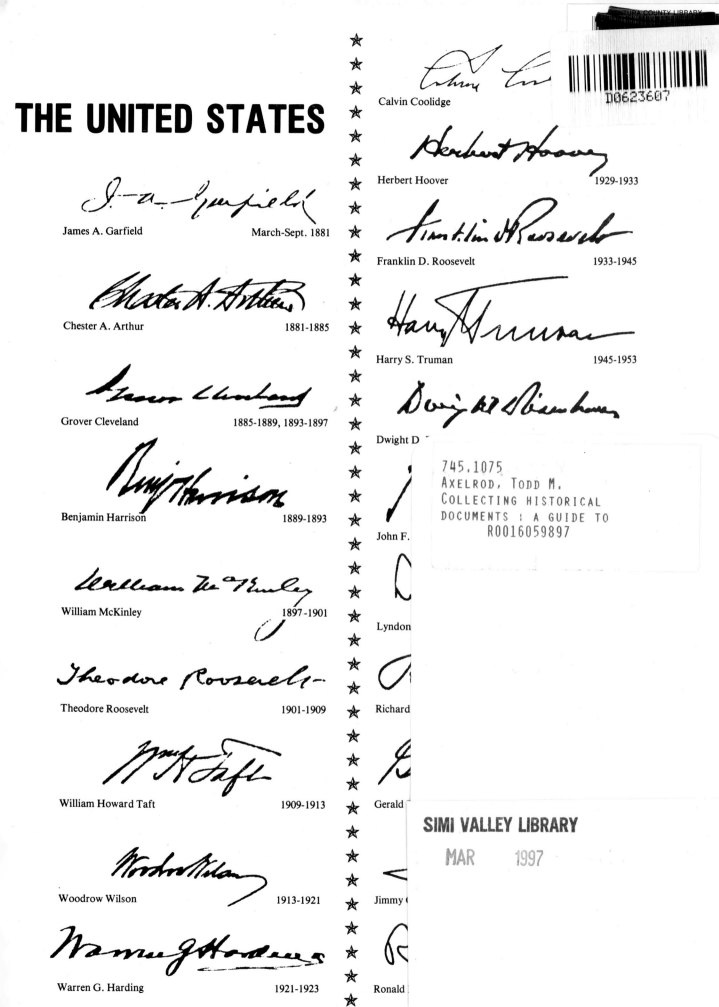

James A. Garfield — March-Sept. 1881

Chester A. Arthur — 1881-1885

Grover Cleveland — 1885-1889, 1893-1897

Benjamin Harrison — 1889-1893

William McKinley — 1897-1901

Theodore Roosevelt — 1901-1909

William Howard Taft — 1909-1913

Woodrow Wilson — 1913-1921

Warren G. Harding — 1921-1923

Calvin Coolidge

Herbert Hoover — 1929-1933

Franklin D. Roosevelt — 1933-1945

Harry S. Truman — 1945-1953

Dwight D

John F.

Lyndon

Richard

Gerald

Jimmy

Ronald

ISBN 0-86622-008-9

Distributed in the UNITED STATES by T.F.H. Publications, Inc., 211 West Sylvania Avenue, Neptune City, NJ 07753; in CANADA by H & L Pet Supplies Inc., 27 Kingston Crescent, Kitchener, Ontario N2B 2T6; Rolf C. Hagen Ltd., 3225 Sartelon Street, Montreal 382 Quebec; in ENGLAND by T.F.H. Publications Limited, 4 Kier Park, Ascot, Berkshire SL5 7DS; in AUSTRALIA AND THE SOUTH PACIFIC by T.F.H. (Australia) Pty. Ltd., Box 149, Brookvale 2100 N.S.W., Australia; in NEW ZEALAND by Ross Haines & Son, Ltd., 18 Monmouth Street, Grey Lynn, Auckland 2 New Zealand; in SINGAPORE AND MALAYSIA by MPH Distributors Pte., 71-77 Stamford Road, Singapore 0617; in the PHILIPPINES by Bio-Research, 5 Lippay Street, San Lorenzo Village, Makati Rizal; in SOUTH AFRICA by Multipet Pty. Ltd., 30 Turners Avenue, Durban 4001. Published by T.F.H. Publications Inc., Ltd. the British Crown Colony of Hong Kong.

COLLECTING
HISTORICAL DOCUMENTS
A Guide To Owning History

Todd M. Axelrod

Todd Michael Axelrod, Founder and Executive Director of The American Museum of Historical Documents.

Treasures of history displayed for viewing as well as for purchase.

6

Above: The American Museum of Historical Documents, Chartered, The Fashion Show Mall, Las Vegas, Nevada.
Below: The American Museum of Historical Documents, Chartered, The Dallas Galleria, Dallas, Texas.

Dedication

The world is divided into two camps:

The "I could have's"

and

The "I did's"

This book is dedicated to the precious few in number represented in the latter who dominate the rolls governing innovative progress, who are the architects of the future.

Acknowledgments

This is where I could very easily get into trouble so I have asked my assistant, Shari Thomas, to write this page. I know I will leave out some very important people or risk not properly identifying their respective roles. We thank all of the following people (in alphabetical order) for their most needed help and assistance:

Ruth Alexander
Benny Brassfield
Lynn Bussey
Larry and Pat Campbell
Ruth and George Canvasser
Charlie
Bernadette Cross
Frank Fay and the Boys
Edith Greene
Ethelmae and James Haldan
Robert Hirst
Gregory Janson
Shari Krasner
Cassandra Lane
Rita Lere
Maggie Long

Dick Lund
Dana Merrill
Gerald Newman
John Petersen
William Pitzelle
Stanley J. Richmond
Pamela J. Ring
Rochas
George and Helen Sanders
Sandra Sax
Kay and Jim Sheets
Charles Snow
Anthony Travers
Marianne Vieregg
Peggie Weston

Contents

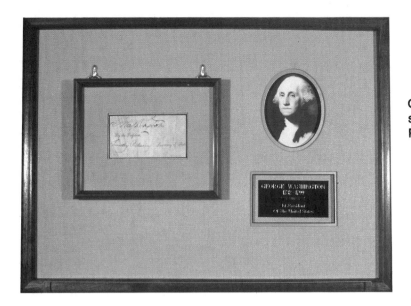

George Washington's clipped signature from a document as President, 1796.

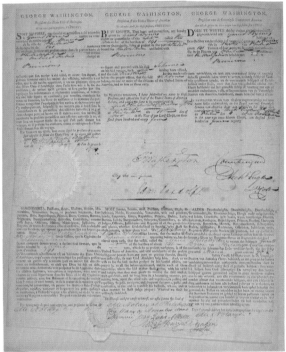

Document (prior to framing) signed by President George Washington.

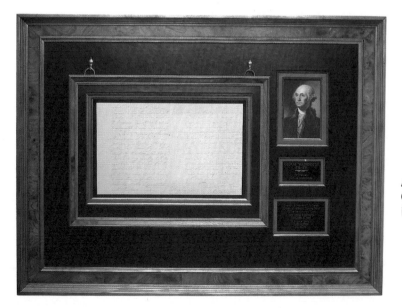

Autograph letter signed by George Washington, Commander-in-Chief, Revolutionary War.

Document signed by George Washington as head of Potomac Company.

An indenture dated August 27, 1740 leasing 345 acres of land by Lawrence Washington, elder half-brother of George Washington. The yearly rental was to be one ear of Indian corn payable on the Feast of St. Michael. The land was an integral part of the tract that was later to become known as Mt. Vernon.

Presidential appointment signed by President George Washington (presently owned by prominent collector).

The author with Charles Hamilton, leading documents expert.

Preface

Did you ever think that you could own the Emancipation Proclamation, Mark Twain's critique of his critics, Groucho Marx's hilarious application to the Friars Club, Albert Einstein's letters on the atomic bomb and his divorce, the Gershwin brothers' travelogs, the Treaty of Paris, or a painting lesson written by Frederic Remington? Well, you can. These are just samples of historical documents. They are pieces of history written by history makers.

Historical documents are collectibles. They are either one of a kind pieces or have highly limited editions. This is because a historical document serves to evidence a particular experience in history or personalizes a history maker. As a result, these documents are unique in content and precious in quantity.

Historical documents have been around for as long as history itself, yet their popularity as collectibles has come into its own during the last 10 to 15 years. Only recently have efforts been made to make the public know that historical documents can be owned privately for affordable prices. In fact, the value of historical documents has steadily appreciated as awareness has grown. And value is expected to skyrocket by the end of the 1980's. Historical documents, then, are similar to undervalued growth stocks—and therefore the best time to purchase them is now.

You don't have to search archives or libraries to find historical documents and you don't have to be rich or be an institution to own them. You simply have to have an interest in some facet of mankind's story which has special meaning to you—be it politics, literature, music, history, the arts, sports or the sciences; plus a desire to be part of the exciting world of collecting—to experience owning an "original"—spending leisure time finding history at auctions, with dealers, in rare bookstores, in flea markets, with fellow collectors.

This book is here to guide you through the process of becoming a collector of historical documents. That process is composed of a number of logical and progressive steps which start at a planning and self-education stage and take you to an acquisition and maintenance stage. It's an approach which I have developed through my experiences as an avid collector and as founder and executive director of The American Museum of Historical Documents. Since the process has been tried and proven true, I believe it to be a practical and useful approach to collecting which both the first-time purchaser and the experienced collector can easily apply and appreciate. You'll also find this book to be a handy reference.

So read on and learn how you can capture moments in time. Learn how to be a collector who owns history.

Presidential signature of John Adams.

Document signed by President John Adams.

To all Persons to whom these Presents shall come,

GREETING.

The American Academy of Arts and Sciences established by a Law of the Commonwealth of Massachusetts, at a Meeting held the Ninth Day of November One Thousand Seven Hundred and Ninety Six for the purpose of promoting the design of their institution, elected the Rev. David Tappan D.D. a Fellow of their Society, and have granted unto him all the rights and privileges of a Member.

And In Testimony thereof have affixed their Seal to this certificate, and caused the same to be duly attested.

Attest

Eliphalet Pearson
Benjamin Dearborn

John Adams President
Joseph Willard Vice Presid.

Appointment (prior to framing) signed by President John Adams.

14

Document (framed) signed by
Thomas Jefferson as Secretary
of State.

Document (unframed) signed by
Thomas Jefferson as Secretary
of State.

Signature of Thomas Jefferson as President.

Autograph letter, discussing portrait of James Madison, signed by
Thomas Jefferson.

Introduction

By the time I was sixteen years old I had been trading stocks for my own account for four years. The richest man in the world, J. Paul Getty, wrote a book entitled *How to Be Rich*★ which was to have a substantial impact on my life.

First, I have invested (?) hundreds of thousands of dollars in tax shelters in oil and gas exploration and have come to the conclusion at the venerable age of 34 that I lack whatever talents, instincts, and luck are required to be successful in this area.

Secondly, and much more importantly, were the concepts espoused by Getty not just in making a buck in oil exploration but also in being successful *period*. I strongly recommend this book to anyone willing to invest $2.95 in their future growth.

I never had the good fortune to meet Mr. Getty. He's gone; but for those willing to take the time and effort, his writings provide all of us some great guidelines, principles, and insights into success—precepts which have been quite important to the author.

When I attended New York University as a night student, I began working as a tax clerk for a major New York City bank. My boss had started with the bank before the Crash! He sat me down one day and said, "Todd, I started with this bank 40 years ago as a runner making $17 a week. Today I am a Vice-President making $30,000 a year. Keep your nose to the grindstone and someday you too can achieve the success I have enjoyed." A month later, I resigned. I started to invest in

small brownstones in Greenwich Village. By graduation I had made over $150,000 from buying and selling brownstones. I was (I thought) the next J. Paul Getty—but in real estate.

I was so sure that everything I touched would turn to gold that when I came up with the idea that *what this country needed was a central market place—ala New York Stock Exchange—for real estate*, I threw myself and my small fortune into it full force. The year was 1973; I was brave, naive, inexperienced, young, and *wrong*. By December 1974 I was broke, $175,000 in debt, and looking for a new beginning. I started working for Paine Webber Jackson & Curtis as a securities brokerage trainee. After five or six months, I was called into my manager's office and told, "Either you resign or I will have to fire you!" "Why?" I asked with astonishment. "Someone downtown read your original employment application and came to the conclusion that you are a bankruptcy candidate. Paine Webber does not have bankruptcy candidates working for it."

Nine years later, I have retired from the securities business—a self-made multi-millionaire. I never did go bankrupt; it sure would have been a hell of a lot easier if I had though. Thank you, Paine Webber!

Probably the most important lesson learned during my Wall Street career was the concept of searching for tomorrow's spectacular performers by research, common sense, and an understanding of relative value analysis.

---

*Published originally by Playboy Press in 1965. Currently available from Jove Books: The Berkeley Publishing Group, 200 Madison Avenue, New York, NY 10016. No. 0-515-07397-0.

When I made the decision to focus my energies on American historical documents, I had come to the following conclusions:

1. People are tired of "manufactured" collectibles. When a company takes $5 worth of silver, stamps it into a coin or medallion, says they are limiting production to 25,000 coins, and sells this for $75, I can't really understand why anyone would buy one! This concept includes collector plates, lithographs, "original replicas," and *rare* stamps and coins where thousands of identical pieces are created.

2. The art market fills an important requirement for people to create an exciting and interesting living and working environment. But lithographs are really just facsimiles of the artist's *original* work which have been signed (often on blank sheets of paper).

3. Ninety-nine percent of Americans assume that all letters of, say, Lincoln, Washington, or Einstein are locked up in the Smithsonian Institute, the Library of Congress, or the National Archives. And yet given the opportunity to understand that they can own *original* historical documents, they love them—they want them—they buy them.

4. Investment-grade American historical documents is the best collectible of unique one-of-a-kind treasures still within the reach of the middle class. The fact that you can buy an example of Abraham Lincoln and George Washington together for the price of a "good" LeRoy Neiman lithograph tells me that we have properly directed our investment of more than $4,000,000 in documents from April 1983 to January 1984!

The (investment) window is open right *now*. It won't be open long. I believe that by 1995 we will look back at today's price levels the way we look back at the official standard price of gold ten years ago at $35 an ounce. Each generation has its opportunity of a lifetime. My grandfather *could* have purchased Miami oceanfront for $100 an acre. My father *could* have purchased Chagall original oils for $1000. We can buy original Lincoln's and Washington's at today's low price levels, and *I am*!

There will always be those who would want to wait for validation from the marketplace—when you see that the investments have and are appreciating dynamically and your next-door neighbor and barber (hair stylist) are *also* taking the plunge. Unfortunately, on Wall Street I learned that when you go for a haircut and your barber (hair stylist) is touting stocks, it's time to short the hell out of the market. You can't have the *comfort* of universal corroboration and still take advantage of the *truly* great opportunities. I have made my decision—my investment. The reader will have to make his own.

Todd M. Axelrod
Las Vegas, Nevada
27 January 1984

Land grant signed by Thomas Jefferson, President, and James Madison as Secretary of State.

Ship's papers (unframed) signed by President James Monroe.

Document (prior to framing) signed by President James Madison.

Land grant signed by President James Monroe.

Above, left: Military appointment signed by President John Quincy Adams. **Above, right:** Military appointment (framed) signed by President John Quincy Adams.

Military appointment (unframed) signed by President Andrew Jackson.

Land grant signed by President Andrew Jackson (now in private collection).

Chapter I
Why You Should Be A Collector of Historical Documents

Collecting historical documents is an interesting, informative, and financially rewarding pursuit. In this chapter, we will discuss the varied types of historical documents available, acquaint you with the people who collect these unique pieces of mankind's story, and, exploding the myths that have kept this field a relative secret, detail the benefits of collecting.

HISTORICAL DOCUMENTS: A WORKING DEFINITION

Mention historical documents to a friend, and chances are that he or she will think you are talking about the Declaration of Independence or an important treaty. The world of historical documents includes much more. Although a basic definition is an original or official paper relied upon as the basis, proof, or support of something relating to, or having the character of, history, historical documents include memorabilia from all areas of the human experience—from the theatre and other arts to medicine and science. Here is a listing and description of the primary components that make up the world of historical documents. You'll find that there are many forms to each component—and with so much variety there's sure to be a subject and historical document to appeal to your interest.

Components and Forms of Historical Documents

1. *Autographs* are original pieces, written or made by the author's own hand, and include:
   * Signatures
   * Letters
   * Drafts
   * Signed Manuscripts
   * Works of Art (drawings, sketches)
   Original, signed pieces are also called "holographs," and these documents are usually the most valuable. Many collectors specialize in collecting only original material, and autographed pieces make an impressive collection.

2. *Manuscripts* are generally defined as intellecual creations such as a piece of writing (including essays) or written music (especially one of considerable size and complexity). Manuscripts are written or typed (as opposed to being printed), and include:
   * Literary Compositions
   * Book Chapters
   * Musical Compositions
   * Typed Letters
   Manuscript materials are available in both signed and unsigned versions. These may include "holographic" works, pieces typed and then signed by the author, or handwritten compositions that are unsigned.

3. *Documents* are forms, usually filled in by hand, and include materials generated by (or relating to) a public figure during his or her lifetime (or for twenty years after death) OR materials relating to a historical event. A sampling of documents would include:
   * Battle Orders
   * Maps
   * Ships' Papers
   * Stock Certificates
   * Land Deeds
   * Commissions and Discharges
   * Requisition Forms
   * Birth and Death Certificates
   * Permits
   * Checks and Bank Drafts
   * Licenses
   * Agendas
   Documents are basically the forms that are

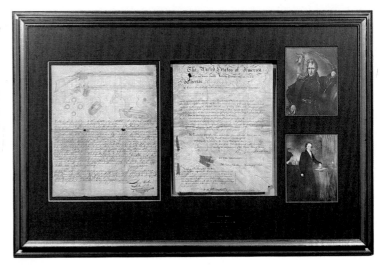

Patent for flintlock rifle signed by President Andrew Jackson and countersigned by Martin Van Buren as Secretary of State.

Ship's papers (framed) signed by President Martin Van Buren.

Ship's papers (unframed) signed by President Martin Van Buren.

Clipped signature of Martin Van Buren.

Four-language ship's papers
signed by President William
Henry Harrison. One of seven
known signatures of Harrison as
President.

Manuscript document signed by
President John Tyler.

Manuscript document signed by
President James Polk.

generated in everyday living—pertaining to both the public and private sectors. Of special interest to the collector are ships' papers—a "passport" issued to all American vessels traveling in foreign waters (except the Mediterranean) detailing the particulars of the voyage and requesting safe passage for the crew. Printed in four languages (English, French, Spanish, and Dutch), these papers were signed by the President and secretary of state.

4. *Printed pieces* are materials printed on letterpresses or by other mechanical means, and include:
   * Handbills
   * Posters
   * Broadsides
   * Playbills or Programs
   * Menus
   * Pamphlets

Printed pieces are usually used to convey information to large numbers of people. Handbills and posters are still used today; in Colonial times, "broadsides" (folio sheets with printing on one side only) were used as public notices. A broadside by Colonial pressman Dunlap, printed immediately after the adoption and signing of the Declaration of Independence, recently sold at auction for $412,500!

5. *Other.* In addition to the types of documents described above, historical documents are available in other forms:
   * Original, Signed Photographs
   * Ancient Vellum Documents
   * "First-Day" Covers
   * Inscribed Books

The wide variety of historical documents provides limitless choices for acquiring a unique and historically significant collection that will increase in value and provide years of enjoyment.

EXPLODING MYTHS: HISTORICAL DOCUMENTS ARE AVAILABLE AND AFFORDABLE

There are two myths associated with historical documents which have discouraged people from considering them as collectibles. The first myth concerns the subject of availability and the second, money.

Availability

We tend to think of historical documents as an invaluable part of our heritage, and we assume that the original documents penned by the men and women who have shaped our world are under lock and key, accessible only to scholars. For the past 100 years, the autograph and manuscript industry has been dominated by historical societies, museums, and a handful of private collectors—contributing to the fallacy that historical documents are inaccessible—"locked up" in the Smithsonian Institution, the Library of Congress, the National Archives, and similar repositories. Nothing could be further from the truth. The truth is that although the number of historical documents is finite, a large selection of these documents is still available to the private collector.

The normal response is one of surprise that any private individual could own letters written by George Washington or a document signed by Benjamin Franklin. And it is only natural to feel amazement to learn that these irreplaceable papers are not only available to private collectors, but that they often receive better care in the hands of a private collector.

Money

Another misconception is that you have to be rich to collect historical documents. Money isn't everything, and although unlimited funds make the towering greats of politics, art, history, literature, music, and science available, a modest budget can still bring the assembly of a fascinating and historically important collection. With a relatively small outlay, you can own signatures, signed photographs, and framed documents of important personages.

There are a number of areas that are especially attractive for the collector with a modest budget. Theatre and sports have made excellent starting points. Another consideration is the pre-Revolutionary War period. The events of 1776 represented the culmination of nearly 150 years of settlement and growth; there is a great deal of autograph material from this period currently available at reasonable prices. Another pursuit is Presidential signatures framed with a photo. These are relatively inexpensive and make for an impressive collection, and they are far less expensive than a handwritten letter or similar document. A Herbert Hoover signed photo, for example, may be purchased for $995, whereas one of his five handwritten letters from his Presidency commands $5,000-$6,000.

COLLECTOR'S PROFILE: WHAT IT TAKES TO BE A COLLECTOR

You don't have to be rich and you don't have to be a scholar to collect historical documents. Collectors are found in all walks of life and from all economic strata. Malcolm Forbes, J. P. Morgan, Queen Victoria, Franklin D. Roosevelt, John F. Kennedy, a doctor in Illinois, an industrialist in New York City, housewives, school teachers, and celebrated attorneys are just a few collectors of historical documents. They, like their fellow document collectors—both past and present—share a common interest in politics, literature, music, history, the arts, and the sciences. Coupled with that interest is their love for collecting—the joy of acquiring original material, the pride of displaying it.

WHY SHOULD *YOU* COLLECT HISTORICAL DOCUMENTS?

How is collecting historical documents different from collecting coins or stamps or art? What are the benefits of collecting historical documents? **Historical Documents are Unique, One - of - a - Kind Collectibles: Pieces that are Never Going to Be Done Again.**

Historical documents, unlike coins and stamps, are unique collectibles that are either one-of-a-kind pieces or have highly limited editions. This is due to the fact that they evidence a particular historical event or personal experience of a history maker—in the hand and/or language of the history maker. This makes these documents original parts of mankind's experience which can never be created again.

Collecting historical documents can be a deeply personal experience for the collector. This is because historic moments and the lives of great individuals have special meaning to the collector. A historical document gets us as close as we can possibly come to those special experiences. Think about it—our acquaintance with those responsible for shaping our world and influencing our thinking is nearly always through secondary sources: books, magazines, television, motion pictures. But historical documents give us first hand insight into our history by sharing the original thoughts, deeds, and writings of the shapers of our world through the letters, documents, and manuscripts they left behind. This is the essence of manuscript and autograph collecting.

There are many reasons why people choose what they collect. Here are some key reasons behind their choices.

HISTORICAL DOCUMENTS RECORD THE STORY OF MANKIND—HIS POLITICS, HIS ARTS, HIS SCIENCES—AND PROVIDE INSIGHT INTO PERSONAL HEROES

For many, the awareness of one's heritage and the people and events which have built that heritage have played an important role in the decision to collect historical documents. Impressive and meaningful collections have been built based upon the focus of one's roots. An appropriate example is the American Presidency, a popular subject of collecting for it combines one's interest in his heritage with his relating to the *person* in the President. When we think of Thomas Jefferson, Abraham Lincoln, Franklin Roosevelt, and Harry Truman, we think of them as individuals who brought personal experiences to the Presidency, experiences with which many can identify. As a collector, you can easily conjure up a score of subjects that relate the man to the position: religion, education, diplomacy, partisan relations, presidential wives, personal tastes, habits, thoughts on any given subject from slavery to tariff regulations — the list is endless.

Insights Into History

Owning a historical document puts a fragment of the life of a personal hero right into our hands. Each of us at some point in our lives has been deeply moved by something we have read, or we have been inspired by a life led to the fullest, or by the adventures of intrepid individuals. The experience of an eighty-five year old gentleman from Springfield, Illinois is a striking example of this point. A surgeon by vocation and training, this man's true love and intellectual pursuit had been the study, understanding, and enjoyment of Abraham Lincoln. While this gentleman had been successful in collecting most of the books written about Lincoln and had amassed an impressive collection of Lincoln memorabilia, he had never ac-

Document signed by President Zachary Taylor, third rarest Presidential signature (now in private collection).

Signature of David Atchinson, who served as 12th President for *one day* between inauguration of Zachary Taylor and expired term of President Polk (now in private collection).

Autograph letter signed by Jefferson Davis as Senator from Mississippi (1850) to President Millard Fillmore.

Military appointment (un-framed) signed by President Franklin Pierce.

Military appointment (framed) signed by James Buchanan.

tually owned anything written in Lincoln's hand. During a visit to The American Museum of Historical Documents, he came upon a Lincoln letter with important Civil War content. His awe of the piece was equaled only by his amazement that he could actually possess such a document. After completing the purchase, he said that this acquisition, while not the most significant that he had made monetarily, was one of his most important. He had never dreamt that he, personally, would be the steward of such an important fragment of Lincoln's life.

Owning a historical document gives us the opportunity to get a glimpse into the personal lives and thoughts of some of the greatest people who have ever lived. Too often we admire outstanding individuals and our heroes for their accomplishments only. Owning a historical document gives us the opportunity to get a glimpse into the personal lives and thoughts of some of the greatest people who have ever lived. Too often we admire outstanding individuals and our heroes for their accomplishments—only to lose sight of their humanity. A historical document can fundamentally broaden our perspective of the human experience . . . mention the name of Albert Einstein, and chances are that you will conjure up images of a reclusive genius, his computer-like mind rapidly calculating possibilities, his mouth spewing forth mathematical formulas. This may, indeed, be one aspect of Einstein, but the staff of The American Museum of Historical Documents was privileged to meet "another" Einstein. We had acquired one of the most remarkable Einstein letters in private hands. This letter, not dated, was to his lover or mistress during his second marriage to Elsie. Not a "Peyton Place" type of document, the selection of the words and the warmth of the letter are a revelation of Einstein's psyche and heart, an incomparable insight into Einstein the human being, Einstein the passionate man. All who have read this letter have been left spellbound and moved.

A letter can reveal much about its author. Ardent outdoorsman, brilliant politician, conservationist, hero of the Spanish-American War, Theodore Roosevelt was truly a rugged individualist. He represented the archetype of virile American manhood, overcoming a sickly youth to become one of the more robust figures in our history. Yet, as we read his letters—especially the ones written to his wife and children—a different kind of man emerges; sensitive, caring, almost feminine in his affection. It makes an interesting contrast to the volatile "TR" leading the Rough Riders over a line of Spanish bayonets.

Another example for consideration is Mark Twain. Under the direction of Robert H. Hirst, the editor of the Mark Twain Papers at the University of California at Berkeley, a seventy-volume text of the papers, letters, and works of the great American author is being published. In compiling material for the text, Hirst found that over half of the letters amassed had never been read by the general public. These letters gave enormous insight into Samuel Clemens and provided concrete evidence of history; the original manuscripts authenticated the published works of Mark Twain.

Professional Association Collecting

Collecting documents for reasons of professional affiliation has also become popular. Doctors may collect letters of Lister, Osler, and Jenner; an attorney may collect the signatures of the Supreme Court Justices; an aspiring writer might collect the signed works of American literary greats. All prove to be valuable and inspiring collections.

There are a number of areas in collecting historical documents which have high growth and return potential. Investment grade Americana is one such area. This includes Presidential material (especially handwritten letters during the Presidency), "founding fathers" (such as Benjamin Franklin), signers of the Declaration of Independence (see Appendix C for a list of all of these signers), and Confederate Civil War material. Additional interest is being focused on black leaders (Martin Luther King, Jr., Booker T. Washington), feminist leaders (Susan B. Anthony), and motion picture stars (especially the "classic" stars such as Lon Chaney, Sr., Greta Garbo, Rudolph Valentino, Marilyn Monroe). A fairly new area, and one that will become increasingly valuable by the end of the century, is participants in the U.S. Space Program. The original seven astronauts, members of the Gemini and Apollo teams, the Skylab and space shuttle crews—all are today's "pioneers."

Historical Documents As Art

In addition to the historical, personal, and investment benefits of owning historical documents, many collectors value their collections for their beauty and decorative appeal. With today's preservation and mounting methods (discussed in detail in Chapter IV), your historical document collection can be handsomely displayed for years of pride and pleasure, the envy of visitors and friends, an exciting alternative to other forms of art.

★★

CHAPTER SUMMARY

1. There are wide varieties of historical documents that will appeal to every interest.
2. Collectors of historical documents share a love of history and the story of mankind, coupled with a desire to own the original material of an individual or event of special meaning.
3. Historical documents are not all "locked up" in museums and archives—they are available to private collectors.
4. It doesn't require a lot of money to begin collecting.
5. Collecting historical documents provides valuable insights into the men and women who have shaped our world.
6. Collecting unique, one-of-a-kind historical documents can yield tangible financial rewards.

Endorsement signed by Abraham Lincoln as a lawyer in Springfield, Illinois, 1842.

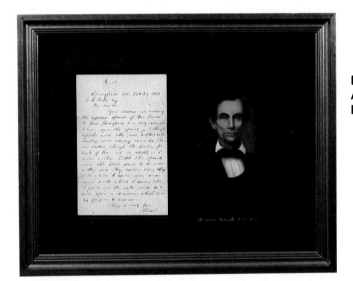

Rare autograph letter signed by Abraham Lincoln, Springfield, Illinois, 1860.

Draft notice signed by President Abraham Lincoln, 1863.

Appointment of Postmaster signed by President Abraham Lincoln.

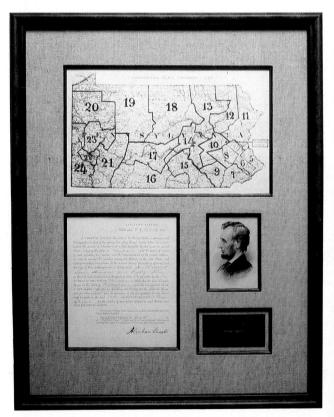

Above, left: Signature of Abraham Lincoln. **Above, right:** Emancipation Proclamation signed by President Abraham Lincoln.

Autograph letter signed by Mary Todd Lincoln, August 3, 1872.

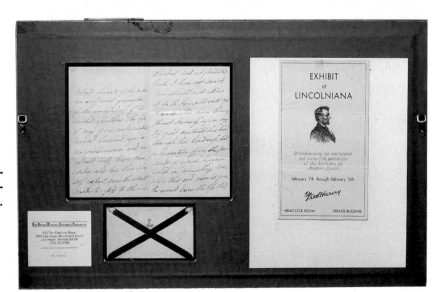

Verso of Mary Todd Lincoln letter revealing supportive material.

31

Chapter II
How To Go About Collecting

You don't have to be rich or scholarly to enjoy autograph collecting. Nor do you have to lurk in concealment, ready to pounce on the celebrity of your choice. All you need is an interest—and the willingness to follow that interest wherever it might lead you. In this chapter, you will see how to go about learning more about the world of historical documents, and how to use that knowledge to develop a strategy for collecting. You will learn how to integrate your strategy and interests into a general plan for a collection, a collection that will provide historical insights and personal satisfaction.

STRATEGIES FOR COLLECTING

A first-time venture into the world of historical documents can be an overwhelming experience for the prospective collector. Confused by the options available—from the many sources of acquisition to the wide variety of materials (often described in terms that might well be a foreign language)—the uninitiated might well decide to give up on the whole idea of collecting. But this needn't happen.

The world of historical documents doesn't have to be confusing. The beginning collector's questions—"What should I collect?", "How do I get started?", "Where do I find documents?", and "What do I do with documents after I purchase them?"—are all easily answered. As in every other field of endeavor, there is a logical progression of steps that will make collecting almost "second nature." These steps are:
1. Become informed.
2. Determine your areas of interest.
3. Develop a plan for your collection.
4. Build a relationship with a reputable professional dealer.

These steps provide a solid foundation for the beginning collector. By following these four basic steps, as detailed in this chapter, your approach to collecting will result in a collection that will appreciate in value, bring years of pleasure, and dramatically document a part of mankind's history.

BECOMING INFORMED
Books

If you are totally unfamiliar with the field of autograph collecting, do exactly what you are doing now—read! This book, for example, will guide you by providing a step-by-step approach to collecting, and there are a great number of other books available (many are listed in this volume) that detail the various areas and aspects of collecting; you should avail yourself of this knowledge. Familiarize yourself with the terms commonly used by autograph collectors (I have included a glossary in this book); the vocabulary of collecting is a simple one, though mystifying to those outside of the field. A working knowledge of the field of historical documents is necessary to provide the background that you will need to make intelligent decisions about your own collection.

In order to effectively plan a strategy for the acquisition of material, it is essential that you become aware of the business of autograph collecting. Familiarize yourself with the autograph market. Learn as much as you can about the ways in which pieces may be obtained (Chapter III discusses sources of acquisition in great detail), and how a variety of factors affects document values. A knowledge of relative values will help you to determine the areas of collecting that correspond with your personal and financial framework.

Contacts

Another way to become informed is through talking with others interested in historical documents. Don't hesitate to engage other collectors in conversation—most are knowledgeable and

Andrew Johnson
signature.

Autograph letter signed by
Ulysses S. Grant.

Casein rendering signed by artist Gutekunst
and President Ulysses S. Grant.

Pardon signed by Presi-
dent Ulysses S. Grant.

Note signed by President Rutherford B. Hayes.

Pardon signed by President Rutherford B. Hayes, 1875.

Appointment signed by Rutherford B. Hayes as Governor of Ohio.

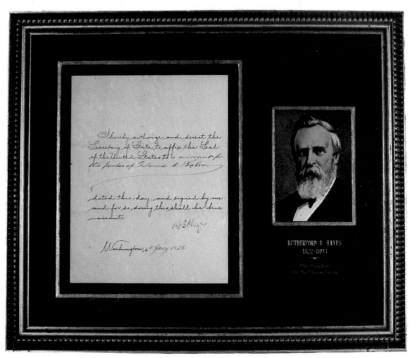

enthusiastic about collecting and are delighted to be of help. Your best source for information and guidance is, of course, a reputable dealer.

DETERMINING INTERESTS

Once you have familiarized yourself with the field of historical documents and the types of material available, your next step toward collecting historical documents is a simple one: decide what interests you. Most collectors are motivated by a specific interest in a person or event. This interest provides the stimulus to seek out documents and gain further insights.

After you have determined your own interest(s), take some time to do a little reading and research on your area of collecting. Become familiar with your subject matter, and try not to pass up an opportunity to expand or deepen your understanding. This knowledge will be of great help when acquiring materials—many forgeries (discussed in detail in Chapter III) have been discovered by collectors who have found blatant historical errors or misrepresentation of facts.

Whatever area or areas of collection you settle on, keep a couple of thoughts in mind. First, remember that one thing often leads to another. This is especially true of autograph collecting; though you may begin by assembling Signers of the Declaration of Independence, don't be too startled if you end up collecting naval autographs of the War of 1812—it happens all the time.

Second, don't be afraid to use your imagination. The best collections are those that are meaningful and bring personal satisfaction to their owners, and delving into a relatively unexplored area can bring unexpected results (your collection may shed a whole new light on a previously ignored topic or personality).

PLANNING

In order to effectively plan a strategy for the acquisition of material, it is essential that you answer the following questions:

1. Why do I want to collect? For investment? For personal satisfaction? Or both?
2. What types of materials do I want to collect? Letters? Documents? Framed, signed photographs?
3. What are my financial limitations? Am I willing to spend top dollar for top quality material or must I limit my spending?

Your answers to these questions will greatly affect your strategy. If you have decided to collect for investment purposes, your strategy will be different from that of a collector who is interested in obtaining only the memorabilia of a personal hero. And the other factors involved—availability of materials and cost—will figure prominently in determining how you will go about acquiring pieces.

Before we discuss the basics of planning, let's take a moment and set some general parameters. When someone becomes involved in autograph collecting, the heady excitement that accompanies that first purchase of a desirable autograph often leads the would-be collector headlong into chaos. The utter confusion and financial drain caused by a poorly planned and uncoordinated series of purchases can often discourage the novice collector and stunt what otherwise might grow into a satisfying, lifelong avocation. This "method" of collecting is called the "shotgun" approach, and can be avoided with a little foresight and careful planning.

It is important to begin with an overall plan. That plan may change; you may find yourself led down corridors that you never knew existed. But, at the end, you will have a *logical structure* to your collection, and the manuscripts that you acquire will complement each other to form a meaningful and coherent whole. (You will find your collection to be far more meaningful and interesting if the material is thoughtfully interrelated.)

The importance of planning cannot be understated. One must be careful not to allow one's desires to outstrip one's resources. Before committing yourself to the purchase of an extremely expensive piece of material, consider your options carefully. Would such an expenditure limit your ability to expand your collection? As a brief example: for the price of a single letter written by Josef Stalin in his own hand, you could assemble an intriguing collection containing letters and documents written by most of the political and military figures of World War II. It's a decision that has to be made according to your own interests and desires.

Types of Collections

When planning your overall strategy, you should be aware that there are different types of collections. Collections fall into three basic structures as follows:

1. *The Specific Collection.* The type of collection one most often sees in museums, libraries and other institutions, this type of collection revolves around a single person, subject, or period of history. The basic characteristic of this type of collection is great DEPTH on a single subject.

For instance, it has become customary for presidents of the United States to establish libraries that act as repositories for materials of every sort that concerned their term(s) of office. Examples of these specific collections include the Herbert Hoover Presidential Library (established in 1962) in West Branch, Iowa; the Franklin D. Roosevelt Library (built in 1939-1940) at the family estate in Hyde Park, New York; the Truman Presidential Library (a repository of over five million books and documents) in Independence, Missouri; the Eisenhower Presidential Library in Abilene, Kansas; the John F. Kennedy Library (founded in 1977-1978) in Boston, Massachusetts; the Lyndon B. Johnson Library (containing over 30 million books and documents) located on the campus of the University of Texas in Austin; and the Gerald R. Ford Library on the campus of the University of Michigan at Ann Arbor.

Often, a university will receive a gift of autograph material from an alumnus and use that gift as the nucleus of a specific collection. The University of California at Berkeley has an extensive Mark Twain collection and the University of Texas has accumulated a collection of the works of Edgar Allan Poe.

2. *The Cluster Collection.* This type of collection does not seek the great depth of a specific collection. Instead, it encompasses the material of certain individuals who share a common denominator. Their conjoint achievements might occur in the same historical period—or may span the centuries.

An example of the cluster approach is Harvard University's collection of New England authors. Signers of the Declaration of Independence and American presidents are very popular with cluster collectors. Your own interests might lead you to collect subjects as varied as Revolutionary War financiers, Prime Ministers of England, or managers of major league baseball teams.

3. *The General Collection.* A general collection is similar to a specific collection, but it lacks the great depth of the specific collection. A general collection may cover one area of subject matter (such as sports, arts, or politics), or it may be totally eclectic. Most private collectors hold general collections.

Although your first inclination might be to concentrate on a specific, perhaps narrow area, I suggest that you plan a wider approach; I recommend that you collect in several different areas. In the stock market, it doesn't make a great deal of sense to invest your entire fortune in one stock issue. The same is true of any investment; it makes sense not to place all your eggs in one basket. Don't hesitate to allow your collection to expand tangentially. What many people do is collect in areas that are different but associated.

The collection of Lucius S. Ruder of Clearwater, Florida is an excellent example of a carefully planned collection. Ruder was not preoccupied with collecting for profit, but diversified his holdings as a skilled investor would have done. The result, a magnificent collection of Revolutionary War generals, Confederate leaders—including a vast amount of the materials of "Stonewall" Jackson and Robert E. Lee, leaders of the old Northwest, and Presidents was purchased in 1966 for $382,154.

REPUTABLE DEALERS

When deciding on the type of collection and your overall strategy for collecting, it is best to seek the advice and counsel of a reputable dealer. A dealer can guide and assist you in the most important aspect of collecting—acquiring quality documents. Without this acquisition, there can be no collection, and the fewer mistakes made in this process, the easier it will be to assemble a collection that will bring you satisfaction (and prove of historical importance).

Autograph collecting is subject to the same vagaries of the market as any other collectible. For many years, prominent figures of the First World War were in tremendous demand. That demand slackened considerably after the Second World War, when the major players in that conflict came to prominence. This is easily understandable, since the latter war has a more direct bearing on

Clipped signature
of James A. Garfield.

Signatures of James A. Garfield as President and his
assassin, Charles J. Guiteau.

Document signed by
President James Gar-
field, second rarest
President signature.

Verso of letter signed by Chester A. Arthur.

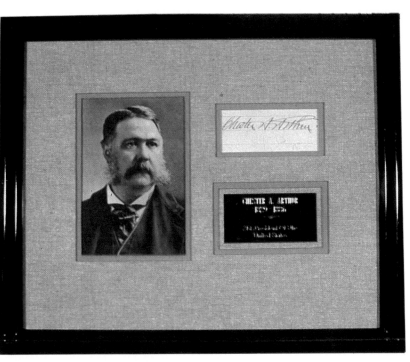

Clipped signature of Chester A. Arthur.

Autograph letter signed by President Chester A. Arthur.

our lives today. Certain areas of collection come into vogue, until interest in the event or individual passes or is supplanted. There are even areas that become "fashionable" for a period of time.

Experienced in handling manuscripts, your dealer will be invaluable in evaluating your needs—and locating documents that meet both your financial and personal requirements (dealer relationships are discussed in further detail in Chapter III).

★★

CHAPTER SUMMARY

1. By following four basic steps, the beginning collector can develop a strategy for acquiring a collection that provides historical insights, personal satisfaction, and investment potential.

2. Becoming informed is the first step toward developing a plan for a collection of historical documents.

3. Determining interests will assist the collector in planning the type of collection desired and help to establish financial guidelines.

4. Planning a collection saves time and money and results in a collection that is integrated and cohesive.

5. There are three basic types of collections: specific, cluster, and general. *Specific* collections are characterized by the depth of the material, *cluster* collections by the theme common to their subjects, and *general* collections fit neither category (lacking the depth of the specific collection and being eclectic at the option of the collector).

6. Using the services of a reputable dealer will provide the collector with the knowledge and expertise needed to begin collecting.

Chapter III
How To Start Your Program

Once you have familiarized yourself with the world of historical documents, have evaluated your interests and developed your general plan, you are ready to begin your program. In this chapter, we will focus upon the basic sources of acquisition of historical documents and acquaint you with the "tools of the trade" that you will use to appraise the values of autographs and manuscripts.

SOURCES OF ACQUISITION

How does one go about the business of actually purchasing autograph and manuscript material? Unless you have inherited a collection or are in the fortunate position of corresponding with the subject of your collection, you will have to rely on the standard methods of acquiring autographs and manuscripts.

Rare bookshops, flea markets, other collectors, and even Aunt Nettie's unexplored attic are all potential sources; autograph auctions are another. But all of these methods suffer from several major drawbacks.

The first four sources represent the "shotgun" approach, and you can waste an enormous amount of valuable time without any guarantee that you will find any manuscript of interest.

The people with whom you will be dealing are not necessarily experts; they are seldom in a position to certify an autograph or manuscript as genuine. This is not to suggest that any deliberate fraud might be intended; in selling what they sincerely believe is a genuine autograph, they themselves may be duped. There has been a dramatic increase in forgeries accompanying escalating autograph values; any collector does well to be wary.

Beware of the friendly fellow willing to sell autographs "freshly" found in the attic trunk of some fictitious aunt. Be cautious when someone offers a manuscript at substantially below market value. Take the time you need to satisfy yourself that what you are buying is the genuine article—if it is, your source will not object to a short waiting period to allow for verification of the document.

REPUTABLE SOURCES OF ACQUISITION

The two most reputable sources of autographs and manuscripts are auction houses and document dealers. Both sources offer guaranteed manuscripts and can provide invaluable assistance to the beginning collector, but there are major differences.

Buying from auction houses

In making first purchases, auction houses are often used by beginning collectors. Autograph auctions can be a great deal of fun, but there are a number of dangers and pitfalls—especially for the novice collector. Pitfalls for a beginning collector to consider in dealing with auction houses are bidding procedures (as in any other type of auction, professionals generally have an "edge," and "hidden elements"—such as dealer pools—may dramatically affect results), establishing the validity of pieces (while a reputable house takes every precaution in offering only genuine material, there is room for error—this is especially true when the auction house does not specialize in manuscripts only), and preservation of purchases (most documents are sold unframed, "as is").

Most auction houses offer illustrated catalogs (available by subscription) that provide detailed descriptions of pieces available at specified sales. Specified sales include "fine sales" where the base prices of items range from $700-$800 and up and "general sales" where the base prices range from $300-$400 and up. Items may be sold individually or in a group (lots).

Descriptions of items often include abbreviations that identify the types of documents available, and a knowledge of these abbreviations

Military appointment (unframed) signed by President Grover Cleveland.

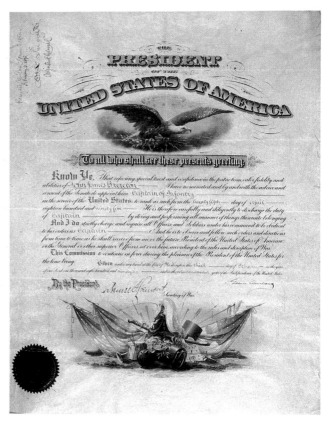

White House card signed by President Grover Cleveland.

Signature of Benjamin Harrison.

Letter signed by President Benjamin Harrison, 1892 (now in private collection).

Land grant (framed) signed by
President William McKinley.

Photo signed by Grover
Cleveland (now in private collection).

Land grant (unframed)
signed by President
William McKinley.

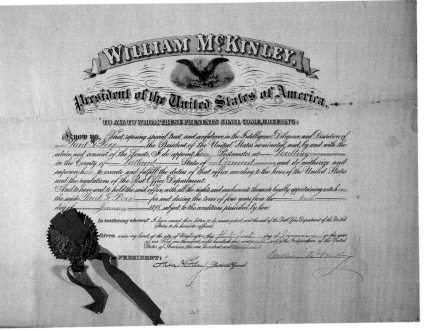

is essential. You should understand that these terms may vary from place to place—sometimes, they will not be capitalized, or a slightly different form will be used. But with this list in hand, and a little deduction, you should be able to decipher any abbreviation.

A.	Autograph
A.D.	Autograph Document
A.D.S.	Autograph Document Signed
A.L.	Autograph Letter
A.L.S.	Autograph Letter Signed
A.Ls.S.	Autograph Letters Signed
A.Ms.	Autograph Manuscript
A.Ms.S.	Autograph Manuscript Signed
A.Mss.S.	Autograph Manuscripts Signed
A.N.	Autograph Note
A.N.S.	Autograph Note Signed
A.P.C.	Autograph Postcard
A.P.C.S.	Autograph Postcard Signed
A.Q.	Autograph Quotation
A.Q.S.	Autograph Quotation Signed
A.V.	Autograph Verse
A.V.S.	Autograph Verse Signed
ca.	Circa
D.	Document
D.S.	Document Signed
fol.	Folio
Hs.	*Handschrift* (handwritten)
L.	Letter
L.S.	Letter Signed (only the signature in the author's hand)
M.O.C.	Member of the Continental Congress (Sept. 1774-March 1789)
Ms.	Manuscript
Mss.	Manuscripts
Ms.S.	Manuscript Signed
N.	Note
n.d.	No Date
n.p.	No Place
n.y.	No Year
p.	Page
pp.	Pages
P.C.	Postcard
P.C.S.	Postcard Signed
Pres.	President
S.	Signed
Sec.	Secretary
sig.	Signature
Signer	Signer of the Declaration of Independence
T.	Typed
T.L.	Typewritten Letter
T.L.S.	Typewritten Letter Signed
T.Ms.	Typed Manuscript
T.Ms.S.	Typed Manuscript Signed
T.N.S.	Typewritten Note Signed
Vol(s).	Volume(s)

When studying these auction catalogs, beware of those that publish "estimates" or predictions of prices that the offered material will bring. These "estimated values" listed in a pre-sale catalog may or may not accurately reflect the true market value of an autograph or manuscript. Often, these estimates prove to be totally meaningless (we will discuss this point in greater detail later in this chapter).

Bidding can be done by mail or in person. Mail bids and sealed bids from the floor are entered into an "order book" from bid sheets on the back of each catalog—the number of the lot or item is entered in the left column, your top bid is entered in the right column. The bidding then goes to "the floor"—the auction room itself. Auction procedures and bidding are discussed at length in *Auction Madness* and *Scribblers and Scoundrels* by Charles Hamilton.

It is important to make yourself known to the auctioneer or one of his assistants before the sale and declare your intention to bid. If you are not known to the auction house, you may be asked to make a small deposit; deposits from new bidders with adequate references are usually waived.

Before bidding, there are several areas that the new bidder should be aware of.

1. Know the terms of the sale. Usually printed on the catalog, these terms include bidding procedures, commissions paid to the auction house (called a "buyer's premium", usually 10%), and whether pieces are guaranteed ("as is" or "at the buyer's risk" indicate that there are no guarantees, and unless you are an expert in autographs, the safest avenue is to employ a reputable dealer to bid for you).

2. Use catalog estimates of value as *guidelines* only. These estimates are "predictions," and may not reflect the true values of pieces offered. Estimates may be too low if the auction house is ignorant of the rarity or desirability of pieces; too high if the seller has asked for a large reserve (minimum selling price) or overestimated demand for items or

if bidders known to bid on only expensive ($10,000-$20,000) lots are expected to appear.

3. Know what you're bidding on. Read up on the lots offered and examine pieces beforehand to see exactly what you're bidding for. In many cases, an overlooked or underestimated document has brought the purchaser many times his or her purchase price.

4. Don't succumb to "auction fever." Your best defense against being caught up in a frantic bidding melee is to remain calm and don't allow yourself to be pressured into bidding. Know your price limitations and stick to them.

5. After purchase, examine your lots carefully to be sure each is intact and that you have received the documents listed.

6. If in doubt about auction procedures in general, contract the services of a reputable dealer. The expertise you will be getting is well worth his or her small commission fee, and may save you from expensive mistakes.

After the auction, a "prices realized" list is sent to subscribers. This list details the items sold, purchaser, and the amount of sale. Remember that these auction prices are not necessarily reflective of general market value. The prices received at auction are often taken as a barometric indicator of the general market in much the same way that the Dow Jones Index can be taken as a general indicator of the stock market, but a variety of intrusive factors can result in a false reading.

For example, attending an auction in New York City in the middle of a blizzard might get you a great deal of material at prices substantially below their true market value—simply because the weather was too inclement for people to attend. In December of 1981, I attended an auction at a major New York auction house at which some very important Margaret Mitchell documents were up for bid. Because I had been in New York for several days and had experienced the effects of the weather, I knew that the usual ten-minute ride by taxi would take an hour, and arrived at the auction well in advance of the sale; many of my competitors from out of town were late or missed the auction entirely. Because of their absence, I was able to purchase the Margaret Mitchell lot containing approximately 70 letters and documents,

many of which had remarkable content relating to *Gone With The Wind*; a purchase made at 75-80% less than the estimated value due primarily to weather conditions!

A short time after my successful bid, a harried executive from the South rushed onto the floor and approached me about the purchase. He had come from Atlanta as a corporate representative solely to acquire the Margaret Mitchell lot. His plane had been delayed by the weather, and he had missed the bidding!

The presence of several individuals intent on buying certain autographs or manuscripts to complete their collections, however, can drive the price of an otherwise ordinary item through the roof. Weather, location, attendance, economics, and the idiosyncrasies of individuals can put a price on an item that might bring half as much—or twice as much—the very next day, if placed for sale on the open market.

Before leaving the subject of auctions, I should mention that there has been a subtle change of direction during recent years. This trend has been drawing the bulk of quality autograph material away from the auction houses and into the hands of private dealers.

Buying from reputable dealers

The expertise and experience of a reputable dealer is a new collector's best "insurance policy" against costly mistakes, so above all seek the advice and counsel of a reputable dealer. In my own experience, one lesson has stood out above all others: it is necessary to get your collection started on the right foot; and without reservation, I feel that the best way to accomplish this goal is through a solid relationship with a reputable, experienced dealer.

Your dealer will be a font of indispensable information and guidance—helping you to get started and afterwards advising you on all aspects of collection. I have helped many people become involved in autograph collecting, and most dealers welcome inquiries and prove invaluable when you are trying to find specific material to complete your collection.

Reputable dealers can be found in several major cities, but unfortunately there is no central clearing house to assist aspiring collectors in finding a dealer. Dealers are often found by word of mouth or through dealer advertisements in periodicals for collectors, but these approaches may not

Thanksgiving Proclamation signed by President Theodore Roosevelt, November 2, 1905.

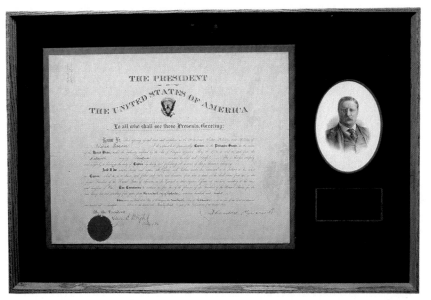

Military appointment signed by President Theodore Roosevelt.

Photograph signed by Theodore Roosevelt.

Appointment signed by President Theodore Roosevelt.

Check signed by
Theodore Roosevelt.

Note signed by
Theodore Roosevelt.

Military appointment signed by
President Theodore Roosevelt.

always be satisfactory—collectors may have interests or needs that require the services of a specific dealer. The American Museum of Historical Documents will be happy to refer collectors to specialized contacts, and we may be reached at 1-800-634-3125.

The use of reputable dealers benefits the collector for the following reasons:

1. *Prices.* The price of documents is set by each dealer (although you should bear in mind that individual dealer prices for similar material can vary depending on the dealer's current stock, his own liquidity, his knowledge of the subject at hand, his costs when the document was acquired, and his personal estimate of the market).

2. *Guarantees.* Items are guaranteed to be genuine, and there is a money-back guarantee if items are not what they are represented to be. Guarantees are only as solid as the dealership that offers them, so the dealer's reputation and financial standing are of utmost importance.

3. *Auction expertise.* If you should see an item in an auction catalog that you simply MUST have, let your dealer bid on it for you. This is what he does for a living and you can be assured of professional assistance.
   ONE WORD OF CAUTION: Treat your dealer as you would have him treat you; deal with him in a straightforward manner. I have seen collectors secretly contact a number of dealers, seeking to purchase an item as cheaply as possible. Often the net result is an artificially created, competitive market—with a good chance that the price will be driven up by the purchaser unwittingly bidding against himself!

4. *Materials.* The sheer volume of material can be confusing and overwhelming. When you pick up a dealer's catalog, you will see all kinds of material for sale: manuscripts, letters, diaries, notes and notebooks, printed documents, handbills, posters, circulars, simple signatures, and books autographed or inscribed by the author. These offerings are often accompanied by a resume of the contents (and always a detailed description of the condition). Ask your dealer's advice; he knows your overall plan and can suggest materials to enhance your collection.

5. *Personal service.* Dealers offer mailing lists and maintain "want lists" for collectors who wish to purchase specific pieces. At my own dealership, The American Museum of Historical Documents, our staff of traveling agents bids worldwide to acquire documents and manuscripts for interested individuals.

We also offer an "approval" service to collectors, whereby they may examine materials before purchase. All documents sold by The American Museum of Historical Documents are carefully preserved and beautifully mounted and framed to ensure years of value and enjoyment.

The dealer is also an asset (and ally) to the collector in terms of awareness of specific pieces and potential investment values. The novice collector, unaware of market fluctuations and the reasons for variable prices, may overspend for a piece or, worse yet, pass up valuable finds through inexperience. The experience of a dealer, for example, can help to avoid errors in the following areas:

Coincidence. This is a case of "mistaken identity" due to duplicate names. Don't be overanxious to round out your collection by jumping at the first name that you see—be sure it's the right man! There were over four dozen men—many prominent in the American Revolution—who shared the name of John Adams. Style, date, and handwriting must be compared to ensure accurate identification. Your best protection against this kind of error is knowledge, and besides your dealer's expertise, the following books containing facsimiles of the handwriting of historical figures will prove helpful: *Facsimiles & Forgeries: A Guide to a Timely Exhibition,* William L. Clements Library, 1950; *Autographs of Prominent Men of the Southern Confederacy and Historical Documents,* Cumming & Son, 1900; *The Book of the Signers: Containing Facsimile Letters of the Signers of the Declaration of Independence,* William Brotherhead, 1861; *American Literary Autographs from Washington Irving to Henry James,* Herbert Cahoon, Thomas V. Lange, and Charles A. Ryskamp, 1977; *The Book of Autographs,* Charles Hamilton, 1978; *The Guiness Book of World Autographs,* Ray Rawlins, 1977; *From the White House Inkwell: American Presidential Autographs,* John M. Taylor, 1968.

Change. The penmanship of historical figures may change for a variety of reasons—Lord Nelson lost his right arm and completed later pieces with his left hand; the scrawl of a diplomat crippled by arthritis may hardly be compared to his youthful hand. If you are going to use a facsimile, try to find one that comes closest to the same time period as the document that interests you. Your dealer will be happy to assist you in this effort.

Concealment. Concealment of an author's true identity can be either intentional or unintentional; differing styles of writing, use of noms de plume, or deliberate failure to sign a letter can all add to the confusion. Illegibility is often a problem; such notables as Napoleon Bonaparte, John F. Kennedy, J. P. Morgan, and Louis Brandeis signed with unreadable scrawls. Many collectible individuals write with a script barely decipherable by an experienced expert.

Sometimes a problem is caused by an author's custom of identifying himself by means other than what we commonly refer to as a "signature." Lacking an alphabet, Indians often used pictograms—which are designs or drawings—as signatures. James MacNeil Whistler often used a small butterfly.

In other cases, monarchs of certain historical periods simply signed "I, the King." Sometimes, a signum (a design often found in the shape of a cross, containing the owner's identity) was used; in other instances a monogram was employed—the majority of which might be drawn by a scribe, with the signer contributing in some small way afterwards. Between 1400 and 1600, many monarchs used a "sign manual," a kind of abbreviated signature.

A paraph is another method of concealment. Defined as "a flourish made after or below a signature, originally to prevent forgery," the paraph is sometimes used as part of a signature or stands alone in place of a signature. Occasionally, the signature is affixed by a secretary, with the author contributing only the paraph (Charles Dickens used an elegant paraph).

Surrogate signers. In many cases, works are signed by secretaries or scribes—Franklin Delano Roosevelt had seven secretaries authorized to sign his name! Another historical example is Jefferson Davis' wife, Varina, who expertly imitated his handwriting (using small variations to indicate that it was her own). Knowledge and expertise is needed in this area to ensure that the signatures that you are collecting are indeed the ones attributed to the greats represented.

"Legitimate forgers." Mechanical means of reproducing signatures have also been used—from the polygraph of Thomas Jefferson to metal and rubber stamp facsimiles (Andrew Johnson used this method of affixing signatures after sustaining a hand injury, and most of his Presidential material was "signed" in this manner). Today's mechanical devices include the Autopen and Signa-Signer, and while the signatures generated by these means are acceptable from a legal point of view (hence the name "legitimate forgers"), these facsimiles have very little value to collectors.

The Autopen reproduces a signature from a plastic matrix, using a pen. The Signa-Signer is capable of faithfully reproducing an individual's handwriting on any type of paper at any angle, with any type of point. This machine is so deviously clever that real expertise is required to discern reproductions from an authentic autograph. Many public figures complicate the verification process by either denying use of these machines or by simply remaining silent. President Kennedy was among the first to take advantage of these "ghost writers," and all subsequent presidential papers should be carefully scrutinized for authenticity. From an autograph collector's point of view, these mechanical signatures are not more valuable than a rubber stamp facsimile.

If you are interested in pursuing this subject further, I would recommend that you read Charles Hamilton's *Big Name Hunting* or *The Robot That Helped to Make a President.* Mr. Hamilton has devoted himself to the discovery of mechanical signatures and is probably the world's foremost expert on the subject.

Copies. It may seem paradoxical to discuss the merits of different types of copies in a book dedicated to the collection of original autographs and manuscripts, but the collector needs to be aware of copies and how they are classified. Admittedly, no copy can compare in value or appeal with a holographic original; but copies may still be of great interest to a collector who would otherwise be unable to complete or fill in his collection.

In the realm of autograph collecting, there are two kinds of copies: "work copies" and "fair copies." There may be considerable "gray area" that exists between the two categories, and the easiest way for the average collector to distinguish between fair and working copies is to determine the purpose of the copy: what was the original intent? The work copy is created to record a body of

Taft Dynasty—three political Tafts on one paper during respective terms of office (now in private collection).

White House card signed by President William Howard Taft.

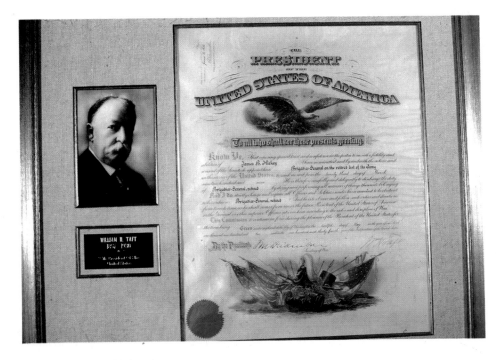

Document signed by President William Howard Taft.

50

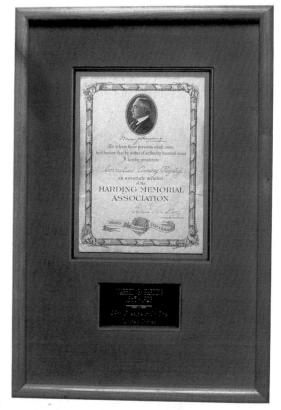

Top, left: Photograph signed by President Woodrow Wilson and the White House Press Corps. **Above:** Document signed by Warren G. Harding.

Appointment signed by President Woodrow Wilson.

Document signed by President Warren Harding.

information. It should not be confused with a draft, which is an original autograph. The work copy is often compiled from an original draft in order to provide a permanent record. A working copy may have been produced on a colonial letter-press, a Xerox copier, or a piece of microfilm; it may have been copied by hand by a secretary. The intent is to create a duplicate record for purposes of preservation.

The "fair copy" is created with a different purpose in mind. One might think of fair copies as having been created with the intent of "being suitable for framing." A poet might write out or type and sign a favorite poem for a friend or autograph collector. A composer might write out a few bars of music. These are actually copies of the original, but they have the potential of becoming valuable if the original is destroyed. The fair copy is usually the more valuable of the two. An example of a fair copy was created in 1824 when John Q. Adams, then Secretary of State, authorized the printing of a commemorative copy of the Declaration of Independence, commissioning W. J. Stone, a printer and engraver. Stone's copper plate (two years in the making and now housed in the National Archives) produced an exact replica of the historic document, and two hundred copies were printed on parchment and distributed to the living ex-Presidents, State governors, members of Congress, and fifty-four colleges. To date, William Coleman, treasurer of the Manuscript Society, has managed to locate a total of only 18 copies; the locations of the remaining copies are yet to be determined.

FORGERIES

Not to be confused with copies, forgeries are deliberate attempts to pass off bogus documents as originals. Fear of forgeries is a healthy fear to have, and the old adage applies: forewarned is forearmed. As your interest in autograph collecting develops, you'll be introduced to a very select group of men. While their names—Robert Spring, William Henry Ireland, "Major" Byron, and Joseph Cosey—may not seem familiar to you, perhaps their pen-names will: George Washington, William Shakespeare, Lord Byron, and Abraham Lincoln!

Most of their forgeries were unbelievably transparent, and all of these men were eventually exposed. However, other forgeries were so clever that only the final, audacious fraud uncovered the successful ones that had preceded it. This was the case with Ireland, who produced "genuine" Shakespeare manuscripts. He managed to dupe James Boswell, the British Museum, and a number of prominent experts. His counterfeits were not only accepted by this impressive group, they were applauded. Producing a play, *Vortigern*, supposedly penned by Shakespeare and never published, proved to be Ireland's downfall—apparently, he was a far better forger than playwright. (See *The Great Shakespeare Forgery*, Bernard D. N. Grebanier, 1965).

With a little study (interesting books on this subject include *Literary Forgeries*, James Anson Farrer, 1907 and *Scribblers and Scoundrels*, Charles Hamilton, 1968) and some attention to detail, you should be able to detect most forgeries. A little time invested in researching your field of interest can yield substantial dividends. Many forgeries contain blatant historical errors: discussions of events yet to occur, references to concepts not yet born, or even correspondence between individuals whose lifetimes did not coincide. The majority of forgeries are surprisingly amateurish and easily detected.

Equipped with the basics of detection, most of us can weed out the obvious fakes. There are several blatant characteristics of many forgeries that can be spotted immediately:

1. *Handwriting.* It is helpful if you are familiar with the handwriting of the subject. Remembering that handwriting can change through a person's lifetime, how does it look? Countless facsimiles are available for study and comparison—don't hesitate to make use of them (close scrutiny with a magnifying glass can reveal a multitude of sins).

2. *Perfection.* Watch out for autographs that look "too perfect." Most letter writers do not try to create a framable masterpiece of calligraphy. Writing with a hand that is characterized by speed and laxity, they avoid the even perfection of the forger. Most people write with an even pressure; most forgers do not—they are too busy striving for the perfect imitation.

3. *Content.* Do the overall features of the subject autograph conform with other examples that you have seen in terms of style, mode of expression, and personality? George Washington's letters, though interesting and

readable, tend to be overly formal, even a bit stilted; a chatty letter from George to Martha discussing the thrills of picnicking on the Potomac is a likely forgery.

4. *Physical components.* Aside from the content and style of the autograph, look at the physical components. An examination of the paper, ink, envelope (if there is one), and postmark can provide vital clues. Though it is still possible to acquire the writing implements and paper authentic to a number of historical periods, most forgers do not bother.

Many forgers do not know that envelopes did not come into use until the 1840's. Prior to that time, letters were simply folded to create a flap that could be sealed with wax; the address was written on the verso side of the letter. The years 1860 and 1861 saw the invention of aniline ink and woodpulp paper (see Appendix A), and documents of these materials that are dated prior to 1860 are obvious frauds.

Each of us is a unique individual with an original mind and personality expressed with a singular script. Sooner or later, even the most sophisticated of forgers makes a revealing misstep. An in-depth education on detecting forgeries can be acquired by reading *The Law of Disputed and Forged Documents,* Jay Newton Baker, 1955; *Suspect Documents: Their Scientific Examination,* Wilson R. Harrison, 1958; *Forgery Detection: A Practical Guide,* Wilson R. Harrison, 1963; and, *Scientific Aids For the Study of Manuscripts,* Reginald Berti Haselden, 1935.

The better forgeries can be detected only by an expert. Even then, final exposure of a fraud may rest on comparison by association with other material, rather than strictly on the basis of the forged document alone. The best protection is the one that I have stressed throughout this chapter: buy only from a reputable source and make use of your dealer's expertise. If, by some chance, the documents you purchased are not exactly what they were represented to be, any good dealer is more than happy to refund your money.

The Art of Self-Appraisal

As you begin acquiring documents through the sources that we have mentioned, you will want to learn more about collecting and using your collec-

tion as an investment. If you are unfamiliar with autograph values, you may find it helpful to have an understanding of how values are placed on autograph material. We are not talking about investment values here (these are usually dependent on the laws of supply and demand), but rather about the basic *components* of value (we are going to assume that the item is authentic; if it is a forgery, it isn't going to have much value).

Autographs are quite different from other types of collectibles; each one is unique. In one case, any material penned by an individual is extremely valuable. In another case, only material penned during a certain period of an individual's life commands a high price. For instance, letters written by generals during war years or by politicians during their terms of office are much more valuable then letters penned before or afterwards.

There are four major components of value: age, content, rarity, and condition. *Age* deserves a special mention at this point because people commonly associate age with value. This is not necessarily the case. For example, I have a very good friend whose father and grandfather were in the real estate business in northern New England for many years. The grandfather began the practice of collecting old deeds, and the father continued the tradition. Recently, the grandson showed me a small, old-fashioned steamer trunk, completely filled with notebooks containing old handwritten deeds dating back to 1750. He asked me to appraise them, as he was considering selling the collection.

It was my sad obligation to inform him that the old steamer trunk would probably bring more at auction than the would-be treasures it contained. Like many people, my friend was under the impression that there is a direct relationship between age and value.

Unfortunately, all the time and energy put into his grandfather's and father's collection yielded only what pleasure they personally derived from it. There are few items less interesting to an autograph collector than a simple land deed, unless that deed is associated with more meaningful material.

A RULE OF THUMB: Age alone is a crucial factor only if the material predates the mid-17th century (in Europe, the year is 1400).

Content is the "backbone" of value. What does the letter say? What does it reveal about the author? To whom is the letter addressed? A note

Check signed by Calvin Coolidge.

Land grant (framed) signed by President Calvin Coolidge.

Typed letter signed by Calvin Coolidge as Governor of Massachusetts; includes quill pen (now in private collection).

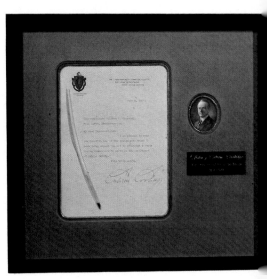

Land grant (unframed) signed by President Calvin Coolidge.

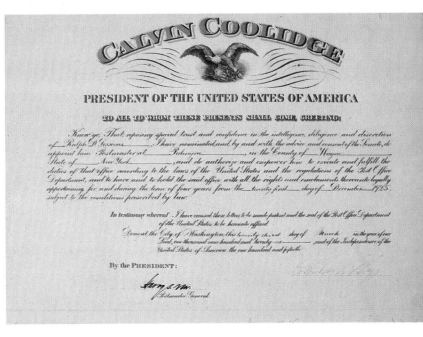

Photograph signed by Herbert Hoover.

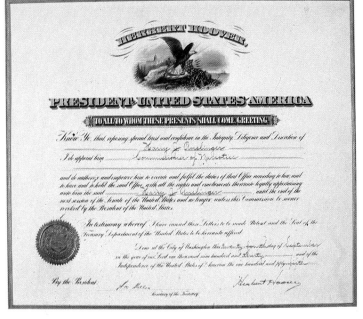

Military appointment (unframed) signed by President Herbert Hoover.

Land grant signed by President Herbert Hoover.

Autograph letter signed by President Herbert Hoover (now in private collection).

from Franklin D. Roosevelt declining a dinner invitation does not compare with a letter to the Secretary of War detailing the President's dissatisfaction with the prosecution of the war; a signed note from Abraham Lincoln declining a routine dinner party does not compare in terms of value or interest with a letter to General McClellan, chiding him on his conduct of the campaign.

With MOST autograph material, the better the content, the higher the relative value. But as with all generalizations, there is an exception to this one. Your choice of area and type of collection will, to a great extent, predetermine the importance of content. A couple of examples:

A collector in Las Vegas who is a movie buff collects signatures, beautifully matted and framed, including the original handbill and a brief history, of Oscar-winning stars. His is a splendid example of a cluster collection and makes a magnificent display. His main interest is in a complete set; letters would have no bearing on his collection.

A good friend of mine, who is a judge, collects the letters of Chief Justices of the United States Supreme Court. They are framed and hung on the walls of his office and home, providing a constant source of pleasure and inspiration. A simple signature on a piece of paper would hold no interest for him.

The same will hold true for you. The type of collection you assemble will determine the importance of content *to you*.

Rarity is a more subtle attribute. In order for rarity to enhance value, it must be accompanied by demand. There are many autographs that are scarce or hard to find, but they remain comparatively inexpensive because demand is so low. Other autographs are scarce and hard to find, but they can be extremely expensive because of the heavy demand.

In another instance, an autograph may be plentiful, but the demand is so great that all material coming onto the market is immediately purchased at exceptional prices. Lincoln is a case in point. Although there is a tremendous volume of Lincolniana, his is perhaps the autograph most universally sought. Lincoln documents with any interesting content are expensive and difficult to obtain. So, rarity must always be associated with demand, in order to have an effect on value.

The fourth factor, *condition*, is an obvious one. A manuscript in good condition will bring a better price than one in poor condition. Again, this factor must be taken in conjunction with the others: the signature of Button Gwinnett (a signer of the Declaration of Independence) is so rare and the demand is so high that condition becomes of less importance.

In evaluating an autograph, all four factors must be taken into consideration. They are so intimately interrelated that any appraisal must consider them jointly.

One point to keep in mind is that the autograph market, like any market, can become glutted. This is usually the result of the hoarding of letters and manuscripts of living persons. When the person dies and mercenary impulses get the best of recipients of these materials, documents are "unloaded" on the market—replacing the relative scarcity of these materials with an oversupply. In time the supply is absorbed and market values will stabilize, but it is important that you remember this phenomenon—especially when dealing in historical documents of living or recently deceased persons.

Another point affecting values concerns an interesting fluke in the marketplace. In recent years, with the increasing number of collectors, there has been an increased demand for one-page letters. A one-page letter with good content will generally realize a much better price than a longer letter with similar content by the same author. A little investigation shows that people are not only collecting in greater numbers than ever before, but that their collections are not going into steel safes or safety deposit boxes—they are going on display in the collector's home and office. Single-page letters are easier to frame or display, hence the increased value for a single-page letter.

It takes a great deal of experience and seasoning to be able to appraise autographs and manuscripts, so don't hesitate to avail yourself of your dealer's expertise. Your own sense of values will grow as you become more involved with collecting—it is a natural function of buying and selling.

Learning how to acquire and evaluate historical documents is only the beginning of a unique experience in collecting. In Chapter IV, we will discuss the ways to preserve and display your collection and introduce you to the scholars and historians to whom your collection may prove of interest.

★ ★

CHAPTER SUMMARY

1. Historical documents may be obtained from rare bookshops, flea markets, other collectors, and personal "finds," but these methods represent a "shotgun" approach and may or may not result in manuscripts of interest.

2. Auction houses are often used by beginning collectors to acquire manuscripts, but prices realized for pieces may not represent true value.

3. Reputable dealers are the collector's best "insurance policy" against costly errors and provide guidance and expertise to collectors.

4. Coincidence, change, concealment, surrogate signers, and mechanical means of reproducing signatures have a great effect on manuscript values.

5. Copies may be considered to fill in or complete a collection, and fall into two categories: "work copies" and "fair copies."

6. Collectors should be wary of forgeries, but there are a number of ways to detect forgeries. Dealer expertise can help the collector to avoid purchasing bogus documents.

7. There are four major components of value: age, content, rarity, and condition. In evaluating material, all four factors must be taken into consideration.

8. Appraising autographs and manuscripts takes a great deal of experience and practice. Availing yourself of a dealer's expertise is the best policy.

Appointment (unframed) signed by President Franklin Roosevelt.

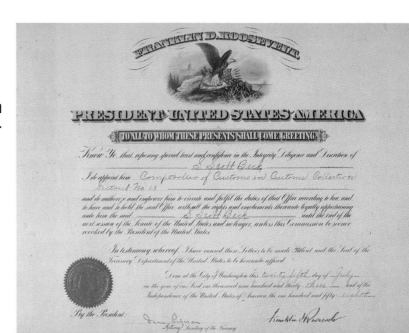

Below, left: Autograph letter by President Franklin Roosevelt thanking a small child for a 10¢ contribution to the March of Dimes (now in private collection). **Below, right:** Photograph signed by Franklin D. Roosevelt.

Above, left: Electoral vote document—the "license" for the Presidency of Franklin D. Roosevelt—signed by several important politicians (including Harry S. Truman). **Above, right:** Card signed by Franklin D. Roosevelt as Governor of New York.

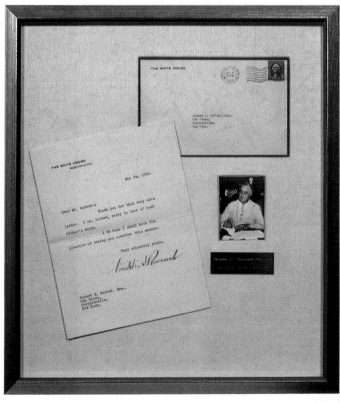

Typed letter signed by Franklin D. Roosevelt, with envelope.

Chapter IV
Maintaining Your Collection

Now that you have begun collecting, you have started on an exciting adventure in history. Collecting historical documents brings with it both joys and responsibilities: the pleasure that your collection will provide to you and others, the responsibilities of the stewardship of irreplaceable fragments of history.

In this chapter we will discuss the enemies of historical documents and show you how to guard your precious manuscripts against the ravages of time. We will also focus on exciting new ways to display and enjoy your collection and introduce the scholars and historians who may find your collection to be of great significance.

You Are the Curator

Once you have expended the time, energy and funds to acquire an autograph or manuscript, you become its curator. Its care and management become your responsibility—not simply to protect your own investment, but also to safeguard and preserve a valuable and irreplaceable fragment of history.

By the time an autograph enters your possession, it may have survived decades or centuries of abuse, carelessness, and neglect. It might be stained, moldy or infested with insects. Sections of the autograph may have holes burned through the paper from the acidic iron gall ink that was commonly used until relatively recently. In short, your new acquisition may be in desperate need of some TLC.

It is my recommendation, however, that the individual collector NEVER attempt to remedy any of the above situations himself. Only an experienced conservator has the knowledge and vast skill required to make repairs and restorations without damaging the manuscript.

Whether you decide to display your collection in your home or office (we will discuss methods of presentation later in this chapter) or simply

choose to store your manuscripts, there are certain safeguards which must be maintained in order to protect your manuscripts from damage. The major enemies of manuscripts are:
* Chemicals
* Light
* Insects
* Humidity
* Mold
* Improper Handling

Chemicals. One of the greatest threats to paper is chemicals. Damage caused by chemicals is insidious because the influence of chemicals is seldom immediately apparent—chemicals work over the course of time, the damage unnoticed until it is too late. Manuscript paper is more often than not acidic—as are many of the inks that were commonly used. Placing the paper in close contact with many materials can begin a slow chemical reaction that will eventually destroy your precious document.

This reaction can be initiated by a variety of materials — many commonly used to store or preserve documents by the beginning collector. Ninety-nine percent of all adhesive materials (including adhesive tape) and other paper products may be acidic (manila folders purchased to preserve manuscripts are often the source of serious damage). Even clear plastics pose a danger — many plastics are acidic.

Light is another enemy of manuscripts. Direct sunlight and unfiltered fluorescent light are dangerous sources of ultraviolet radiation. These rays cause paper to be desiccated and faded or stained. Regular household bulbs or incandescent bulbs do not generate ultraviolet rays, but they do generate heat, which can be just as damaging to a fragile manuscript.

Possibly the most common threat to manuscripts comes not from voracious *insects* or wandering rays of ultraviolet *light,* but rather

Top, left: Typed note signed by Harry Truman. **Top, right:** Photograph signed by Harry Truman. **Middle:** Photo signed by Harry Truman to Charlie Clark. **Bottom, left:** Appointment signed by President Harry Truman.

Harry S Truman
President of the United States of America.

To all who shall see these presents, Greeting:

Know ye, that reposing special trust and confidence in the Integrity and Ability of Edward Mount Webster, of the District of Columbia, I have nominated, and, by and with the advice and consent of the Senate, do appoint him a Member of the Federal Communications Commission for the unexpired term of seven years from July 1, 1942, and do authorize and empower him to execute and fulfil the duties of that Office according to law, and to have and to hold the said Office, with all the powers, privileges, and emoluments thereunto of right appertaining unto him the said Edward Mount Webster, subject to the conditions prescribed by law.

In testimony whereof, I have caused these Letters to be made Patent, and the Seal of the United States to be hereunto affixed.

Done at the City of Washington this nineteenth day of March in the year of our Lord one thousand nine hundred and forty seven and of the Independence of the United States of America the one hundred and seventy first.

By the President:

Harry Truman

Dean Acheson

Acting Secretary of State

Program signed by Dwight Eisenhower and Mamie Eisenhower.

Photograph (swearing in for second term) signed by President Dwight Eisenhower.

Document signed by President Dwight Eisenhower.

from *heat* and *humidity*. Too much humidity and the *mold* spores that are commonly found everywhere will run rampant; too little humidity, and your manuscript will be lifeless and brittle. As we have noted, the paper that old manuscripts are written upon contains acid salts which require just a small amount of water to begin the process of deterioration. The end result is a manuscript so brittle that it breaks with even the gentlest handling.

Even if a manuscript appears in excellent condition, it can quickly deteriorate as a result of improper storage and careless handling. So how *does* the collector protect his manuscripts? There are basically two answers: buy from a dealer who specializes in preserved manuscripts or become more aware of those elements that can affect historical documents and learn to take precautions to guard against them.

At The American Museum of Historical Documents, all documents are carefully preserved and mounted to museum specifications before sale. This includes encapsulation in acid-free Mylar (documents are sealed in using a special acid-free glue approved by the Library of Congress) and mounting on 100% ragboard backing in the frame to keep pieces acid-free. Instead of glass, UF-3 plexiglass (scientifically designed to stop ultraviolet rays from penetrating and fading pieces) is used in the framing.

> *Note:* At The American Museum of Historical Documents, all pieces are guaranteed and mounted using state-of-the-art methods (these methods are detailed and pictured in Chapter VI). Beware of framed pieces of dubious origin; a piece that has been framed isn't necessarily preserved.

When considering the preservation and mounting of documents, don't trust every framer to be aware of all the factors involved in framing a manuscript. Unless he is experienced in the handling of autographs and manuscripts, he will not be aware of the importance of using acid-free materials, special pastes, and glazing. Don't hesitate to ask questions—and if you're not satisfied with the answers, take your business elsewhere (chances are, a talk with your dealer can provide recommendations for reputable framers).

In dealing with the problems of the care for historical documents yourself, it is essential to carefully store and preserve documents in either acid-free manila folders (acid-free paper products are available if you specify them) or in Mylar sheaths (Mylar is one of the few clear plastics that are acid-free). Fortunately, if acidity is already a factor, there is a solution. There is a process called deacidification, which is used by conservators to neutralize the autograph without causing any damage to the manuscript. A second step can be added to the process to give the manuscript a pH basic reserve against future problems. This is a dangerous process best not attempted by anyone except a trained conservator; at this time there are perhaps three or four people in the United States qualified to perform this process. (Call your dealer if you feel that one of your autographs might require this special process—he will probably recommend a qualified person).

If a document has extensive "foxing" (spotting created as a result of mold or mildew), pieces can also be deacidified. While this process cannot undo terrible damage, it can "inhibit" the aging process. With proper care, the document should look as good 100 years from now as it does today.

If an autograph is stained, torn, repaired with adhesive tape or suffering from insect damage, DO NOT ATTEMPT TO REPAIR IT YOURSELF. Always consult your trained conservator. Processes of restoration and repair involve the use of solvents and special techniques best left to the experts.

The easiest way to deal with the problem of light is to glaze framed manuscripts with Plexiglas UF-3 which filters out ultraviolet rays (or you can filter the light source itself). A couple of things to remember: do not allow the glazing material to directly touch the manuscript—condensation may occur; and never use Plexiglas on a material where there is a possibility that the static electricity in the plastic could draw minute particles from the paper towards itself.

When using light to illuminate manuscripts, NEVER place an incandescent light source inside a display case where heat can build up or close to a manuscript where the same problem can occur.

Ideal conditions for manuscripts consist of a relative humidity of 45% to 55% and an average temperature of around 70 degrees Fahrenheit. Avoid extremes of hot and cold. The best conditions are those with a stable humidity and temperature where air is free to circulate. Obviously, this lets out the basement and attic as storage sites. It also eliminates the bathroom, outside walls of the house and radiator sites as ideal display areas.

Ventilation is essential. Never keep your manuscripts in an airless environment. If you happen to be one of those people who insists on the security of a bank vault, check your manuscripts frequently.

If you decide to simply store your collection, encase the documents in acid-free Mylar and store in the acid-free manila folders. Do not, under any circumstances, store the material upright—this could easily damage the edge of a fragile autograph. Store manuscripts flat in a clean, dry place where air can freely circulate.

Exercise care and caution when handling manuscripts. Keep manuscripts away from dirty fingers, half-filled coffee cups, overflowing ashtrays, and intoxicated persons. And NEVER MARK AN AUTOGRAPH IN ANY WAY—ESPECIALLY TO IDENTIFY IT AS YOUR OWN. Altering an autograph can cause damage or destroy its value entirely.

With the help of experts and some basic knowledge, your role as curator can be an interesting and rewarding one. It all boils down to one simple axiom: use good common sense, and your manuscripts will remain in excellent repair.

DECORATING WITH HISTORY

One of the greatest pleasures of collecting is arranging your autographs for exhibition. A well-displayed collection can be a source of constant pleasure, both to the collector and to those friends and acquaintances who visit his home or office. Invariably, my guests are drawn to the autographs I have on display. The question is always the same: "Are these genuine?" Imagine their surprise and delight to be assured that they are indeed viewing original pieces.

I would urge you to freely display your own collection, as I do mine. Sharing the fascinating contents of my collection has provided a real source of pleasure. There are collectors who encase their treasures in steel sheaths and securely lock them away in a bank vault. I suppose that they slip in from time to time and lock themselves into one of those little rooms provided by the bank. There, in solitude—or perhaps in the company of an envious friend—they peruse their collection like a miser who has just lifted one of his cellar floor boards to count the contents of his cache. The example may be harsh, but I personally have difficulty entombing a living part of history.

My own collection, which contains many priceless manuscripts, is freely exhibited in my home and office. Many of my displays are an education in themselves and bring meaning to history. One such display features a signed copy of the Emancipation Proclamation—one of six copies known to be signed by Abraham Lincoln. This document—a delight to all who view it—is even more precious because of the fact that the whereabouts of the other five copies are unknown (and they may no longer exist!). Imagine locking such a document away!

Methods of Display

When you begin collecting, your collection will consist of just a few pieces. As your collection grows, you will want to arrange it appropriately, with a central thread or theme running through each area of display. The wide variety of historical documents easily lends itself to interior decorating, and historical documents provide *original* beauty. Unlike other collectible art, such as lithographs, historical documents are unique pieces—you won't walk into a neighbor's home and see a duplicate hanging on the wall!

AN INTERESTING NOTE: The American Museum of Historical Documents offers beautifully framed examples of all the U.S. Presidents (though not necessarily written during the presidential term) for under $2,000 each. When one considers that a LeRoy Neiman lithograph (which is only a signed *copy* of an original piece of art) can sell for $6,000 or more (2½ to 3 times the price of a document signed by Abraham Lincoln), it is not difficult to understand why historical documents are a viable alternative to more traditional forms of art.

There are many methods of display. By using your own good taste and imagination, you can create displays that will be a source of inspiration and pleasure to all who view them. Pieces may be framed (using the preservation methods previously discussed) and enhanced by moldings, and hung on walls or placed on pedestals. At The American Museum of Historical Documents, pieces are framed using a variety of mattings (including suede and leather) and moldings. Frames include all types of wood (natural, stained, and lacquered or enameled) and metal, and special in-

Top: Typed letter signed by "Jack" Kennedy, Representative from Massachusetts, with photo of Harvard football team. **Bottom, left:** Photograph signed by President John F. Kennedy. **Bottom, right:** Lease for "Brambletide" cottage on Hyannis Port signed by President John F. Kennedy, February, 1963.

White House photos of Kennedy family signed by Jacqueline Kennedy.

Autograph letter signed by John Kennedy (now in private collection).

Check signed by Jack Ruby, assassin of Lee Harvey Oswald.

terest can be added by affixing another framed document to a larger piece (resulting in a "hinged" piece). I have many framed pieces from The American Museum of Historical Documents hung in related groups—sports figures, literary greats, politicians—and these make for interesting and beautiful viewing.

To complement my framed pieces, I contracted with a local craftsman to build several simple display cases. Constructed from sturdy mahogany, these cases boast Plexiglas shelves which do not obstruct one's vision. The documents displayed are protected by acid-free Mylar folders which in no way detract from viewing the pieces. Certain manuscripts that are of particular interest are set off by resting them on a piece of green felt.

Displays can often become unique pieces of furniture in themselves. There are instances when the significance and value of documents involved warrant special attention and display, and the two examples that follow will give you some idea of the exciting possibilities.

A recent acquisition of mine was the letter written by Abraham Lincoln in reply to Grace Bedell, a little girl who had written to him as an aspiring candidate suggesting that growing whiskers would make him more attractive (and thus more likely to win the election). Since this document is the most important non-political letter written by any Presidential figure in history, I wanted to showcase it in an environment befitting its uniqueness and value, a setting that would provide for the preservation and exhibition of this treasure for many years to come.

At a cost of $4,000, a custom designed and built cabinet and matching table were created from solid mahogany. The cabinet is 35½" high, 17" wide, and 15½" deep, and rests on its matching mahogany table (20½" wide, 19½" deep, and 32¼" tall), and was designed to display the document and related materials to best advantage.

Two doors on the top of the cabinet open to reveal the letter, flanked by photographs (accompanied by a brass identification plate) of Abraham Lincoln and Grace Bedell. All of the pieces are matted with hand-tooled leather to create a rich, elegant display.

Beneath this compartment, in a sloping case with a Plexiglas cover, are four "authenticating" letters (letters written to and from Grace Bedell regarding her letter to Lincoln and his reply). The case may be opened to allow for the closer viewing of the letters (all of which are encased in protective Mylar).

Beneath this case is a spring-locked drawer (opened by a solid brass key) that contains books and pamphlets relating to the Lincoln-Bedell story. Another drawer, cleverly hidden in the mahogany table, can also be used for additional materials.

The beauty and elegance of this fine piece of furniture are exceeded only by the historical value of the materials showcased, and this display will add impact and significance to the home of any collector.

Another important acquisition was a copy of the Thirteenth Amendment to the Constitution. Signed by Lincoln, his Vice-President, his Cabinet, and members of the Civil War Congress, it is possible that this copy could have been Lincoln's own, and was a piece that deserved the best possible protection and a fitting method of display.

It is now protected in a solid rosewood frame that was originally a framed mirror attached to a Victorian dresser. With the glass removed, its beautifully carved lines and burl inserts make an impressive backdrop for the Lincoln treasure. The document and a photo from an original engraving are highlighted against black suede that is accented by brown suede; a small brass plaque describing the document is inset in the top of the frame. The piece is almost six feet tall and approximately four feet wide and makes a spectacular addition to any large room.

A massive piece such as this tends to dominate a room and makes an excellent addition to large offices, boardrooms, and bank lobbies. In fact, I predict that the next major boom in historical documents will occur as a result of corporate art programs. Corporations today spend hundreds of millions of dollars to acquire art for corporate offices and premises, and as the public in general—and executives in particular—become aware of the availability and decorative appeal of historical documents, corporate energies and monies will channel into historical documents (resulting in soaring prices).

Displays make handsome additions to smaller rooms as well, and professional offices are enhanced by the signed portraits or original letters of greats in the field. Signed stock certificates make decorative additions to financial offices; the personal letters of medical pioneers add impact to medical offices.

At home, historical documents make excellent conversation pieces and are often the focal point of rooms. Just be careful not to overcrowd your collection; too many autographs crammed into too small a space can detract from the overall impact. Framed displays can fit into any decor—from Early American to Danish Modern. Rooms furnished in Old West antiques, for example, can be highlighted by a fascinating display of signed Mark Twain letters in wooden frames. (Other documents that may be considered include pieces relating to Lewis and Clark or other pioneers such as Daniel Boone and Davy Crockett or western figures Wyatt Earp and Annie Oakley.)

In contemporary rooms, the addition of a John F. Kennedy piece matted in gray suede and framed in silver makes a striking display, as does a collection of John Paul Jones memorabilia matted in black leather with gold accents and encased in a gold frame. For music buffs, consider the effect of a John Lennon photograph and signature matted in gray and yellow suede and accentuated with a gray lacquered frame.

Music rooms can be dramatically decorated with framed musical manuscripts or photos and letters of great composers and performers, home libraries enhanced by framed pieces of literary greats. And a cluster of sports heroes or movie stars adds interest and appeal to dens and hallways.

YOU'D BE SURPRISED WHO'S INTERESTED: THE ACADEMIC CONNECTION

As you become more involved in autograph collecting, you should become aware of two aspects of collecting that don't usually occur to the novice collector. The first pertains to the historical value of your collection; the second concerns your rights to the contents of autographs in your possession.

The historical value of your collection

Never underestimate the value your specialized collection might have to an inquisitive scholar. One day, you may receive a phone call or a letter from a professor or scholar whose name is completely unknown to you; he may express an interest in an autograph or manuscript in your collection. He may have found your name through a

dealer, or he may have scanned auction catalogs to see where documents that could be of interest to him might be found. Scholars are constantly on the lookout for new information that might affect their field of interest: an unpublished letter to a mistress, the discovery of a politician's unknown debt, or a note written in uncharacteristic anger—all might shed new light on the subject, changing the current interpretation.

An example of this scholarly interest, an endeavor that I personally endorse, is The Mark Twain Papers, a 70-volume work now being published by the University of California Press. Based primarily on a cache of literature donated by the family of Samuel Clemens to the University of California at Berkeley in the 1950's, the goal of Robert H. Hirst, Editor, is to publish *everything* ever written by Mark Twain.

Mark Twain, however, wrote many manuscripts, and a large number are not in the University collection; many were letters sent to different people who knew Mark Twain well, and documents and letters continue to appear—including pieces from people selling collections, finds among family papers, and discoveries of manuscripts left with printers (published manuscripts were owned by the printer, not the author).

In the case of Mark Twain, any document generated by him or about him (during his life or for 20 years after his death) is considered to be historical. This includes pages written by a secretary and signed by Mark Twain, pages of his handwriting (but no signature), and other materials of interest to scholars.

The value of these papers is that they fundamentally change the reader's view of Mark Twain; no one had read half of the letters left by Mark Twain, and these "new" documents increase understanding, provide insights into Mark Twain, the man, and evidence history—describing in detail many events of his day.

The Mark Twain collection—and its supplements from other sources (including private collectors like myself)—has generated a tremendous amount of scholarly interest, and three different authors have completed Mark Twain biographies based upon materials in these files!

The dedication of Dr. Hirst and his staff will ensure that these invaluable vestiges of history will remain available for the benefit of all history lovers. An ongoing effort to raise private funds for the Mark Twain project has been organized, and

To M. O. Carter
With appreciation and all good wishes,

Christmas 1968   Lady Bird Johnson Lyndon B. Johnson

Christmas Card signed by Lyndon B. Johnson and his wife, "Lady Bird" Johnson.

Photograph signed by "Lady Bird" and Lyndon Johnson.

For Tom Fox — with warm memories of fellowship at National City Christian Church — Lady Bird and Lyndon Johnson

Inaugural invitation signed
by Richard Nixon and
Spiro Agnew.

Typescript of Oath of Office signed by
Richard Nixon.

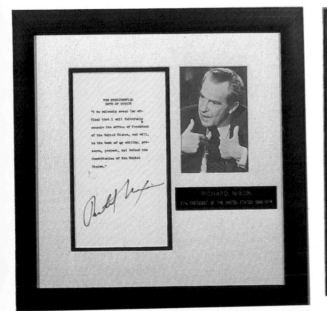

Typescript of Oath of Office signed by Richard
Nixon, dated.

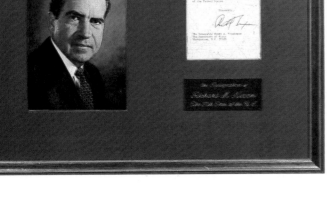

Typescript of Resignation signed by
President Richard Nixon.

your tax-deductible contributions to the Project will ensure that this worthwhile work will continue. All donations received are offered to the National Endowment for the Humanities, which matches them *dollar for dollar* in making grants to the Mark Twain Project. Requests for additional information (or checks made payable to The Friends of The Bancroft Library) may be sent to:

> Mr. James D. Hart, Director
> The Bancroft Library
> University of California
> Berkeley, CA 94720
> OR
> Dr. Robert H. Hirst, General Editor
> Mark Twain Project
> 480 Library
> University of California
> Berkeley, CA 94720

Robert Hirst feels that the work that he and his staff are accomplishing at the University of California at Berkeley only increases the value of the originals. The Mark Twain Papers are not facsimiles but are published text, and Hirst feels that as the work becomes known, public interest in—and demand for—the originals will increase. (To request information or books—three Mark Twain Library volumes are published per year—contact: Sales Department, University of California Press, Berkeley, CA 94720. I want to encourage all collectors of Samuel Clemens to take advantage of this opportunity to share in the in-depth studies of this most provocative genius being compiled by the Bancroft Library.)

Hirst often depends upon the resources of private collectors for material, as do many other academic and historical institutions. If you receive an inquiry into your collection, there are several rules to follow to protect yourself and your collection:

1. Be sure of the identity of the scholar or historian. Call the appropriate institution and verify the credentials of the inquirer and the details of the study.
2. Take steps to maintain control of your manuscripts. Collectors should always decide—and specify to the scholar—how documents can be used. Know exactly what will be done with your material, and then determine whether the original, a photographic copy, or a hand or typewritten transcript may be used. Remember that providing anyone with a copy of an unpublished manuscript lessens your control. To maintain maximum control while permitting access, you can allow the scholar to read your document for substance and content but forbid note-taking or quotation. And NEVER leave your collection solely in the care of the consulting person!
3. Determine the effect on the value of the manuscript. If a copy is requested, check with your dealer to see what effect this might have on the value of your manuscript. Some collectors feel that distributing copies of a previously unpublished manuscript results in a loss of value. But remember that price depends on many variables—supply and demand, rarity, content, condition—and public awareness of your manuscript may actually increase demand (and therefore value). In most cases, I feel that access does not affect the value adversely; quite the contrary, it may help to establish the document's provenance—and involve you in an exciting project.

Collectors' Rights to Content

Historical documents are more than merely unique collectibles with historical significance—they are a legal paradox, a combination of material objects and intellectual creations. Material objects can be possessed, bought, and sold; but what of intellectual thoughts, ideas, and discoveries?

When you acquire a historical document, you become the owner of its *physical components* only; the right to publish (or in some cases, even display) the *contents* of some letters or manuscripts is *not* automatically granted. The contents are protected in many cases by copyright law, and a basic understanding of this law and how it affects you as a collector is essential.

Basically, documents are divided into two categories: "published" and "unpublished." "Published" documents are those whose author had the *intent* to make the works public—marking the work with notice of copyright, depositing copies with the Copyright Office, and taking similar steps to generate quantities of the work. "Unpublished" documents are those such as letters and journals—pieces that were created for personal use only.

Prior to legislation enacted in 1976, statutory copyright law did not apply to "unpublished" letters and manuscripts—the right to control their publication remained, under common law, with the author and his or her estate or heirs. The Copyright Revision Act (passed in late 1976; effective as of January 1, 1978) transformed the former common-law copyright into a statutory copyright. Protection now applies to letters and manuscripts (both "published" and "unpublished"), and guarantees authors the right to control reproduction of their works and monitor certain types of public exhibitions—subject to "fair use."

"Fair use" is a legal term describing the conditions that make the use of a document permissible. These terms include the purpose, character, and nature of the work for which the document will be used (educational pursuits rather than commercial ventures), the amount of the portion of material used (in relation to the work as a whole), and the effect of the use on the potential market value of the copyrighted work. (Limited rights, not available to general users, are often granted to educational institutions, libraries, and archives—provided they comply with prescribed statutory requirements.)

The new statute applies to all works created on or after January 1, 1978 (protection for the author's life plus fifty years) while works created before 1978 but not published by then receive protection from that date (to extend to the later date of either the author's life plus fifty years or December 31, 2002—extendable to December 31, 2027). Works in the public domain before January 1, 1978 are not protected by this act.

It is required to obtain permission from living authors to quote from works or enter into certain types of public display. Because of extensive "gray areas" and possible legal ramifications, your best resource in time of doubt is a competent attorney.

★ ★

CHAPTER SUMMARY

1. As a collector, you are responsible for the preservation and safe-keeping of irreplaceable fragments of history.
2. The main threats to a manuscript are chemicals, light, insects, humidity, mold, and improper handling.
3. With the help of experts and knowledge of manuscript care, your collection will remain in excellent condition.
4. A well-displayed collection is a source of pleasure, inspiration, and educational benefits.
5. There are many methods of display—from simple framing to the creation of fine pieces of furniture—and the wide variety of historical documents available can enhance any decor.
6. In addition to its beauty, your collection can be of significant historical value—and of great interest to scholars.
7. When dealing with scholars and historians, use care to maintain control of your manuscripts and their market values.
8. Historical documents are both physical and intellectual creations, and the collector can only actually own the physical components of documents.

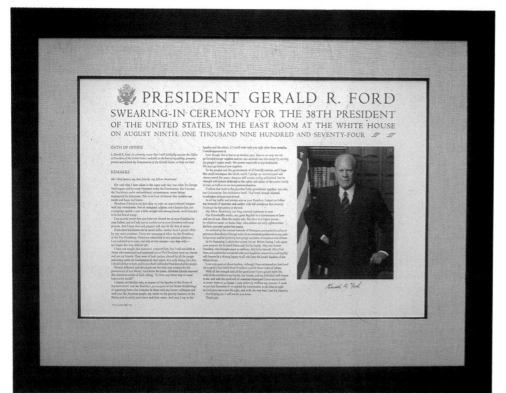

Typescript of Presidential swearing-in ceremony signed by President Gerald Ford.

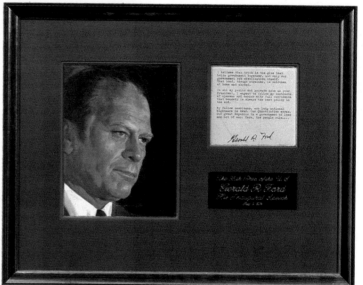

Typescript of his inaugural speech signed by President Gerald Ford.

Campaign photo signed by Gerald Ford; framed with "Win" buttom.

Above, left: Photo and signature (framed) of President Jimmy Carter.
Above, right: Official White House photo and signature of President Jimmy Carter.

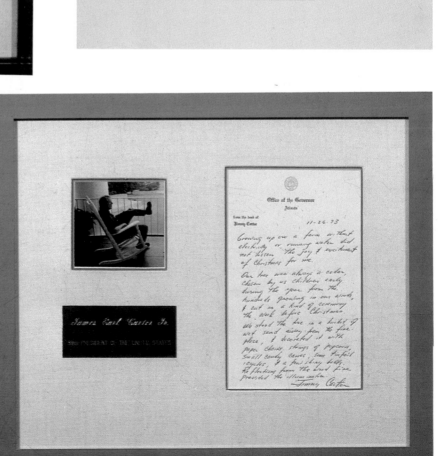

Autograph letter signed by Jimmy Carter.

Chapter V
Components and Forms of Historical Documents: Their Significance In Historical Profiles

In Chapter I, we briefly discussed the joys of collecting—the personal insights, the thrill of owning a piece of history, investment value; in this chapter, we will see how the collecting of historical documents can actually make history come alive—and greatly enhance the lives of collectors. Since most of our discussions thus far have dealt with the details of "collecting," I've included some brief historical sketches to add color to the categories of collecting.

Too often we fail to appreciate the power with which many of these autographs were created. The faded words and yellowed paper deceive us with their age. By being aware of the historical context within which the autograph was written, we are reminded that these autographs were not penned passively, but as an act of living. By learning of the conditions under which a letter was written, we can often read between the lines. If we wish it to be, an autograph can be a living, breathing entity.

You will be reading about a personal interest I have in a certain historical figure. The section entitled "Haym Salomon: A Case In Point" will show you how I was led on a fascinating journey through my involvement with this neglected hero of the American Revolution.

I have also included a short section on the subject of theatre. Though sometimes viewed as a sport for love-struck teen-agers, I collect autographs of the great stars of the silver screen, and I strongly feel that this area of collection should be considered by a serious collector for its variety and investment value.

Other topics for your consideration include history, the American Civil War, literature, music, and the sciences. The wide variety of documents available in these categories add life to any collection, and no matter what your interest—letters, documents, signed musical manuscripts, autographed photos—you will find pieces of interest that are unique and affordable.

Probably the most popular areas of collection in America are Presidents of the United States and Signers of the Declaration of Independence. One friend of mine took a slightly different slant on the subject of Presidents—he collects presidential campaign material. Another friend collects the letters of Presidential wives. I enjoy following the American Presidential races and indulge my penchant for autographs by collecting material of potential presidential candidates (most major figures in the Senate and the House are relatively easy and inexpensive to collect—just watch out for Autopens and Signa-Signers). I choose people I feel may be serious contenders for the nomination at some point in the future. If correct, I strike the motherlode! If wrong, I've still enjoyed myself and put together an interesting political collection with a comparatively small outlay. (For your reference, I have included a table of Presidents of the United States (and their wives), Appendix D, and a list of the Signers of the Declaration of Independence, Appendix C).

The above are just a few examples to help set your thinking processes in action; the variations are endless. Regardless of the areas in which you decide to collect, combine just a little imagination, some careful forethought, and a touch of luck—and I guarantee that your collection will bring you years of pleasure and provide a sound investment.

As we have already noted, the width and depth of your collection is limited only by the scope of your imagination. No parameters exist except the

Postcard signed by Ronald Reagan.

Autograph letter signed by Ronald Reagan; with envelope.

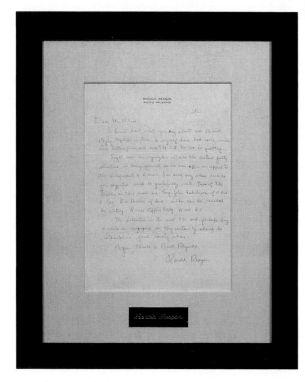

Autograph letter signed by Ronald Reagan.

Autograph letter with notes signed by Ronald Reagan.

Autograph letter signed by John
Jay and Robert R. Livingston,
June 7, 1785.

Autograph letter signed by
Henry Clay.

Autograph letter signed by
Daniel Webster.

ones that you set yourself. On the following pages, you'll find the suggestions for potential areas of collecting. These are meant to serve as examples. Of course, you might find yourself sufficiently intrigued to adopt one or two as your own, but that's a decision entirely in your hands.

Regardless of the subject or area that you decide to collect, whether it's art, movie stars, music, history, or baseball greats, you will find two sets of rewards. The first is the thrill of the chase (inherent in collecting) which ends in the pleasure of ownership. The second is a by-product of the first—an insight that will enrich your life and give you a fresh perspective on a part of the human experience.

HAYM SALOMON: A CASE IN POINT

I must confess that the time I spent in college was not completely devoted to study. I found the subject matter often dreary, seldom relevant. I found history, in particular, to be dry, brittle, and utterly undigestible. Not so any more.

What happened? I met a man named Haym Salomon. I had certainly never heard his name mentioned in conjunction with the founding of our country. But, without question, his contribution was every bit as significant as the contributions of the men who placed their names on the Declaration of Independence.

In 1981, when I purchased a note endorsed by Haym Salomon I never realized to what extent I would become deeply engrossed with the life of this true American patriot. He led me on a journey that opened my eyes to the flesh and blood heroes of the American Revolution. He also showed me the seamy underside of history that the texts don't usually mention—how unscrupulous men abused their high office and how selfless patriotism was rewarded with injustice.

My first contact with Haym Salomon, a name virtually unknown outside of autograph and historical circles, grew out of my interest in making an investment in autographs to diversify my portfolio. The item that I purchased was a promissory note documenting the loan of $30,000 to the United States government (the note itself was made out in the amount of 3,000 pounds sterling, and was signed by Robert Morris in the capacity of Superintendent of Finance on behalf of the United States of America). As a collector and a dealer, this represented a tremendous find as

Haym Salomon is one of the most desirable and rarest of all American autographs.

Little did I know where this ordinary financial instrument, so seemingly devoid of life, would lead me. Not long after I made the purchase, I had the opportunity to relax and study the document. Two items struck me: first, the amount of the loan—for those days it was staggering; second, the note appeared to be outstanding—the debt was still owed! I decided to do a little research. . .my interest had been piqued.

My research yielded some interesting facts. During the first few years of our existence as a nation, there was serious doubt that the United States would last longer than a few years as a Republic. Many thought that we might become a monarchy (Benedict Arnold seemed to favor this form of government). More widespread was the belief that the nation was not, and could not become, a viable financial entity—insolvency might accomplish what thousands of British troops could not.

At the end of the war, the country was exhausted. Years of fighting had taken their toll, spiritually and economically. Washington's biggest problems during the execution of the war were defeating the British Army in the field and finding the money to pay for it—vital funds to pay the troops, to arm, train, and feed them.

During the first year of its existence, the Federal Government was nearly crippled by a lack of hard currency—gold and silver. What precious metals the government had were used to prosecute the war. The Continental Congress had to meet the financial obligations of the government in order to maintain its credibility, but hard specie was in short supply. Remember—much of the population had been Tories, hoping for a British victory. Many Americans had been delighted to wave one of the new flags and cheer Washington's victories, but risking their hoarded gold on an unproven cause was going a little far.

On reflection, one can hardly blame them. The new continental currency had nothing to back it and—in the eyes of the majority of people—was just so much worthless paper. The fear and uncertainty of the times drove hard currency into hiding.

I was intrigued to learn that our post-revolutionary survival was not a foregone conclusion, but rather the result of the selfless dedication and patriotism of a few men, determined to see that

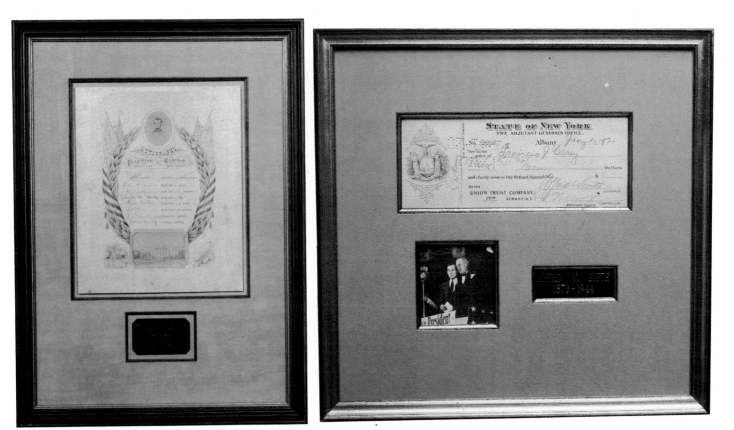

Document signed by Abraham Lincoln's Cabinet and Abraham Lincoln.

Check signed by Alfred Smith.

Typed letter signed by Alfred Smith (now in private collection).

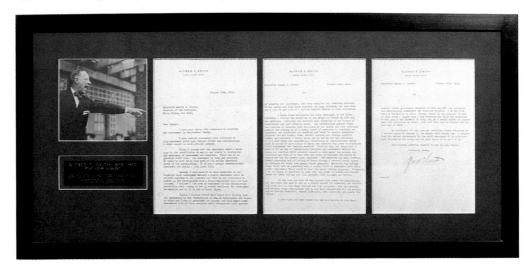

Left: Autograph quote signed by Susan B. Anthony. **Above:** Autograph note signed by Elizabeth Cady Stanton. **Below:** Autograph note signed by Susan B. Anthony.

Photograph signed by Robert Kennedy.

Photograph signed by Chief Justice Charles Evans Hughes and his associates.

Photograph signed by Edward Kennedy.

Typescript of Supreme Court decision signed by Sandra Day O'Connor.

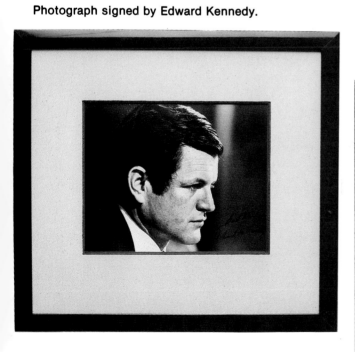

Document signed by John Hancock (now in private collection).

Document dated 1776, signed by John Hancock as President of Congress.

Engraving and document signed by John Hancock.

Autograph letter
signed by John Hancock.

Document (unframed) signed by Benjamin Franklin.

Autograph letter signed by Benjamin Franklin.

Below: Autograph letter signed by Benjamin Franklin. **Right:** Document signed by Robert Morris, 1795, for North American Land Company.

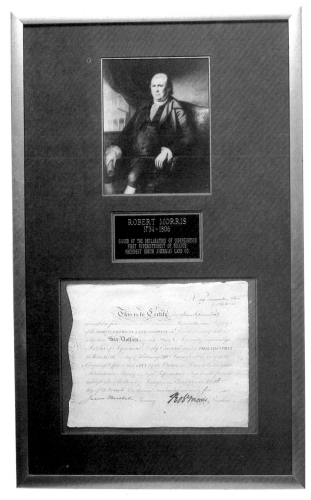

Document endorsed by Haym Salomon and Robert Morris to help finance the Revolutionary War.

Rare autograph note signed by Benedict Arnold.

Official Proclamation of American Ratification of the Definitive Treaty of Paris signed by Thomas Mifflin and Charles Thompson.

Autograph letter signed by John Paul Jones to Thomas Jefferson.

Check signed by General Winfield Scott.

Autograph letter signed by Marquis de Lafayette.

Autograph letter signed by Santa Anna to his son.

Autograph document signed by Samuel
Houston (now in private collection).

Texian loan document signed by Stephen F.
Austin.

The Thirteenth Amendment (Lincoln's personal copy) signed by President Abraham Lincoln and the Civil War Congress.

Close-up of
Thirteenth Amendment.

Autograph document signed by General Ulysses S. Grant (now in private collection).

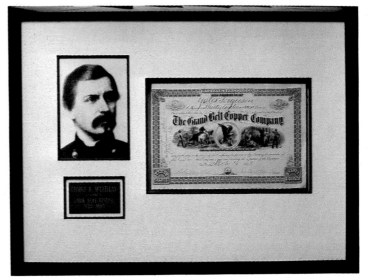

Stock certificate signed by George McClellan.

Autograph letter signed by Edwin Stanton, Secretary of War, 1868.

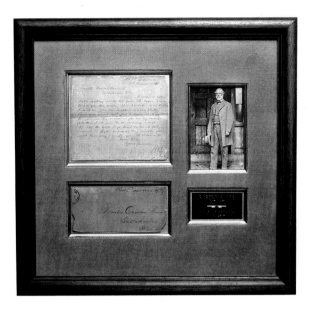

Autograph letter signed by General Robert E. Lee, March 1, 1865 (now in private collection).

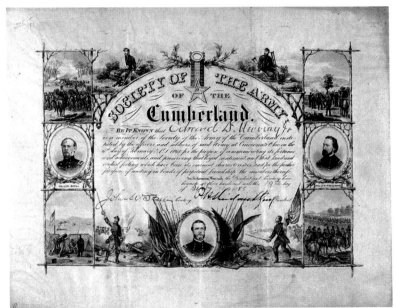

Document (unframed) signed by General Philip Sheridan, Army of the Cumberland, 1886.

Autograph letter signed by Jefferson Davis (now in private collection).

Typed letter signed by
Theodore Roosevelt
discussing sinking of the
Maine, 1898.

Typed letter signed by General John
Pershing.

Photograph signed by General William "Billy"
Mitchell.

Photograph signed by Prime Minister Winston Churchill.

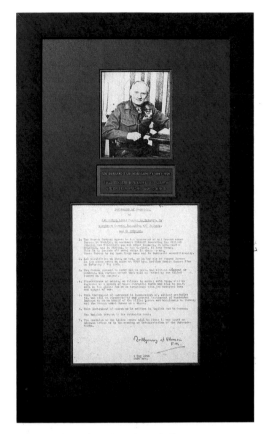

Typescript of surrender of Germany signed by Montgomery of Alamein.

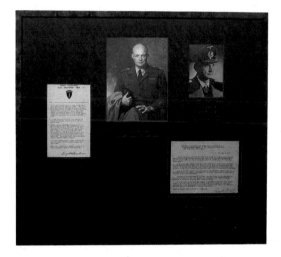

Typescript signed by General Dwight D. Eisenhower and Admiral Karl Doenitz.

Typescript of events during "Battle of the Bulge" signed by Montgomery of Alamein.

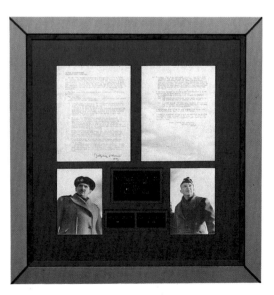

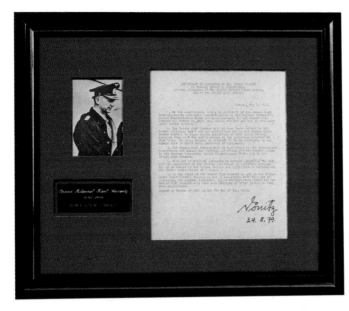

Typescript of German Surrender signed by Karl Doenitz (now in private collection).

Military pass signed by Lt. Col. George Patton.

Military appointment signed by Adolph Hitler and Dr. Joseph Goebbels, Nazi Propaganda Minister.

Typed letter signed by General George Patton with original photo (now in private collection).

Photo signed by
crew of *Enola Gay*.

Photo signed by Gregory "Pap-
py" Boyington, Commander of
the "Black Sheep" squadron
(now in private collection).

Photo of Japanese Surrender signed
by military officials and President
Harry Truman.

Above: Typed letter signed by Douglas MacArthur (now in private collection). **Right:** Autograph quote signed by Douglas MacArthur.

Typed quote signed by General Douglas MacArthur.

Photograph signed by General Douglas MacArthur.

Document (unframed) signed by Queen Victoria.

Document signed
by Napoleon Bonaparte.

Document signed by King Louis XIV.

Document signed by
Napoleon Bonaparte,
translation included.

Typescript of Abdication of King Edward VIII signed by Edward, Duke of Windsor.

Document signed by Dom Pedro I, Emperor of Brazil.

Wedding photo signed by Princess Grace and Prince Rainier.

Engraving signed in Hebrew by Golda Meir (now in private collection).

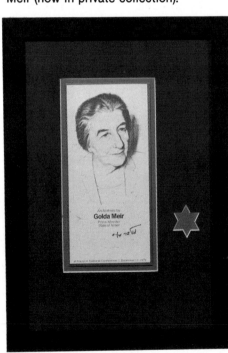

Typed letter signed by Anwar El Sadat on Presidential letterhead.

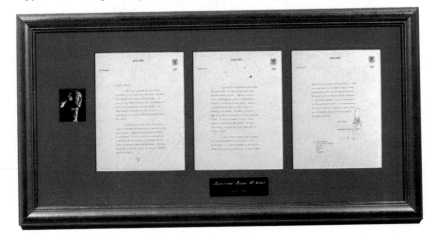

Document signed by
William Penn (now in
private collection).

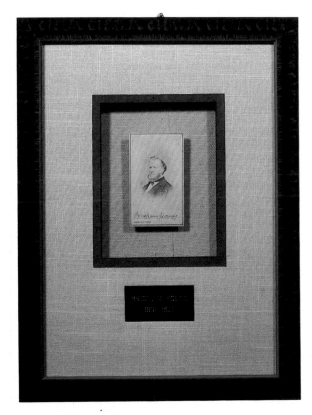

Photograph signed
by Brigham Young.

Signature of Brigham Young framed
with ticket for opening ceremony of
the Salt Lake City Mormon Temple.

American Express Stock Certificate signed by Henry Wells and William Fargo, 1865.

Autograph letter signed by John Jacob Astor.

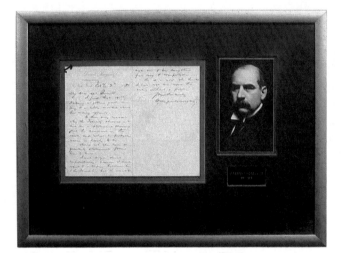

Autograph letter
signed by
J. Pierpont Morgan.

Stock certificate
signed by Cor-
nelius Vanderbilt.

Above, left: Photograph of Howard Hughes, signed. **Above, right:** Signature of Howard Hughes.

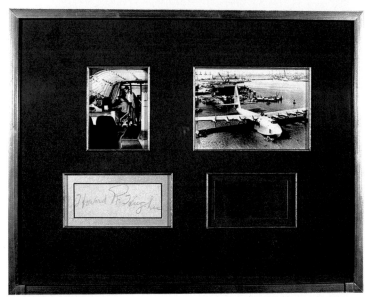

Signature of Howard Hughes framed with photos of the *Spruce Goose.*

High School yearbook signed by Howard Hughes.

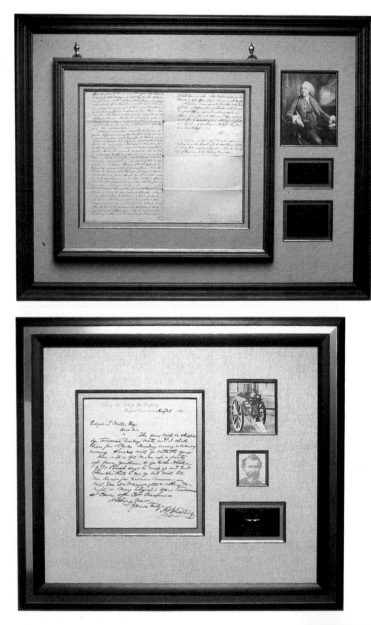

Autograph letter signed
by Benjamin Franklin.

Above and facing page:
Checks signed by Orville
Wright.

Autograph letter signed by Richard Gatling.

Autograph letter signed
by Samuel Colt.

Photograph of Alexander
Graham Bell, signed.

Check signed by Thomas Edison.

Document signed by Thomas
Edison.

Left: Photograph of yacht *Electra*, signed by owner Guglielmo Marconi. **Above:** Note signed by Guglielmo Marconi.

Typed letter signed by Nikola Tesla.

Typed letter signed by Henry Ford.

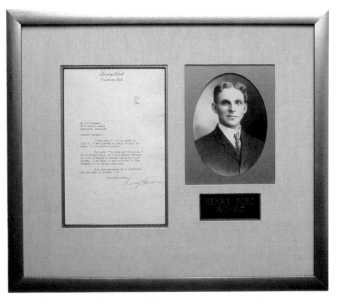

105

Above, left: Signature of Charles Darwin.
Above, right: Autograph letter signed by
Charles Darwin (now in private collection).

Autograph letter signed by Joseph Henry.

Autograph letter signed
by Madame Curie.

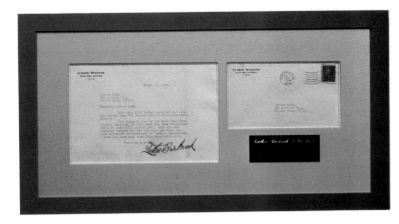

Typed letter signed by Luther Burbank, including envelope.

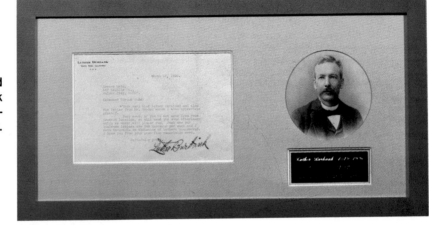

Typed letter signed by Luther Burbank (now in private collection).

Typed letter signed by Albert Einstein.

Autograph letter about his divorce signed by Albert Einstein.

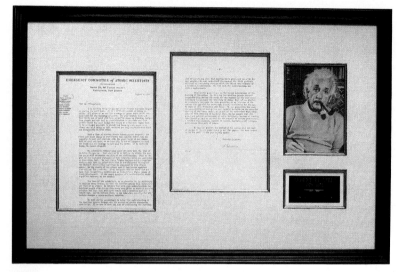

Typed letter signed by Albert Einstein (now in private collection).

Typed letter signed by Albert Einstein.

Rare autograph love letter signed by Albert Einstein.

Autograph letter signed by Dr. Joseph Lister.

Photograph signed by Clara Barton.

Autograph letter signed by Dr. Mary Walker, first female surgeon and only woman to receive Medal of Honor.

"First-day" cover signed
by Dr. Albert Sabin.

Autograph note signed by Sigmund
Freud.

Photograph signed by Carl Jung.

110

Typed letter signed by Amelia Earhart.

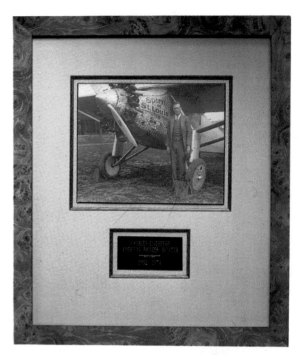

Photograph signed by Charles Lindbergh.

Menu signed by Charles Lindbergh, Cuba.

111

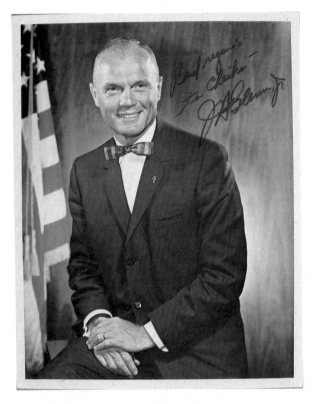

Photo signed by John Glenn, Jr.

Photograph signed by Apollo V astronauts Aldrin, Collins, and Armstrong.

Photograph signed
by Robert Peary,
Arctic explorer.

Typed letter signed by Admiral Richard Byrd, Antarctic explorer.

Autograph note signed
by Meriwether Lewis
and autograph letter
signed by William Clark,
unframed.

Note and letter of Lewis and
Clark framed with leather matting.

Photograph signed by Sir Edmund Hillary (now
in private collection).

Autograph document signed by
Daniel Boone, August 31, 1806.

Document signed by John C. Fremont, March 2, 1868.

Autograph letter signed by George Armstrong Custer, April 5, 1867.

Autograph quote signed by William Cody.

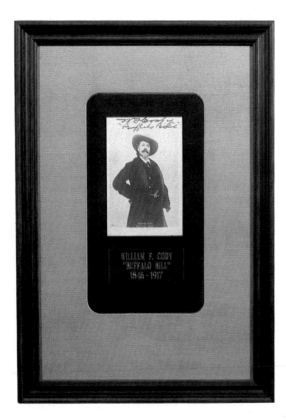

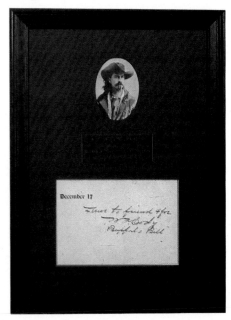

Photograph signed by William "Buffalo Bill" Cody.

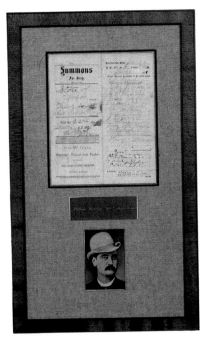

Summons signed by Sheriff "Bat" Masterson.

Stock certificate signed by Pat Garrett.

Autograph letter signed by Wyatt Earp.

Autograph card signed by Cole Younger.

WYATT EARP
1848-1929
Famous Western Lawman

Rare playing card shot twice and initialed by John Wesley Hardin (now in private collection).

Very rare autograph letter (framed) signed by Jesse James.

Autograph letter (unframed) signed by Jesse James.

Autograph note signed by John Wesley Hardin.

Autograph letter signed by
Frederic Remington.

Autograph note signed by Frederic Remington.

Autograph letter signed by Henri
Matisse (now in private collection).

Typed letter signed by
Frank Lloyd Wright, July 9,
1947.

Autograph quote "America" signed by Samuel F. Smith, November, 1832.

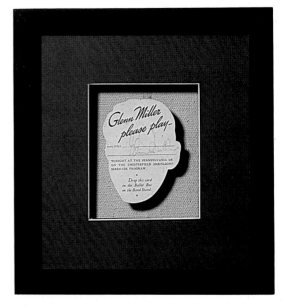

Photo dance card signed by Glenn Miller.

Document signed by John Lennon.

Signature of John Philip Sousa.

118

Musical quote signed
by Leonard Bernstein.

Sheet music signed by Maurice Ravel.

Autograph letter signed
by Niccolo Paganini.

Autograph letter signed by Giacomo Puccini with signed envelope (now in private collection).

Autograph note signed by Richard Wagner.

Autograph letter signed by Richard Wagner (now in private collection).

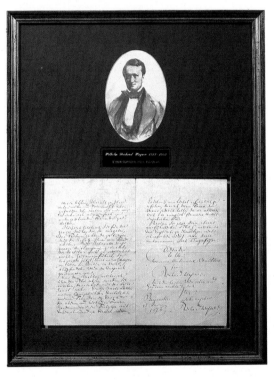

Typed letter with autographed notes signed by George Bernard Shaw (now in private collection).

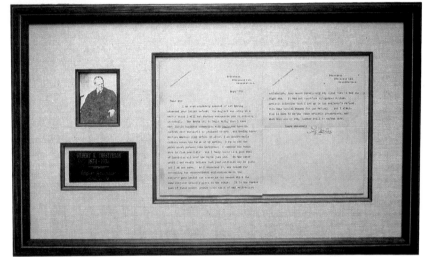

Typed letter signed by G. K. Chesterton.

Below, left: Letter signed by Sir Winston Churchill. **Below, right:** Autograph letter signed by Somerset Maugham.

Check signed by James Fenimore
Cooper (now in private collection).

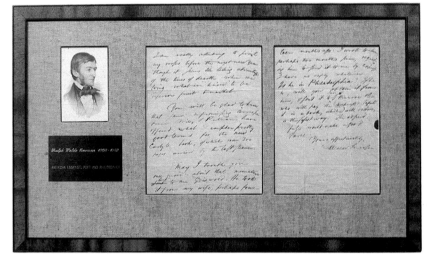

Autograph letter signed by Ralph Waldo Emerson.

Rare signature of
Edgar Allan Poe.

Extremely rare note signed by Herman Melville,
author of *Moby Dick*.

Below and right column: Four autograph letters signed by Samuel Clemens ("Mark Twain").

Above: Photograph signed by Samuel Clemens (now in private collection).

A signed card (top, right), now in private collection, an autograph note (below), and three autograph letters signed by Samuel Clemens.

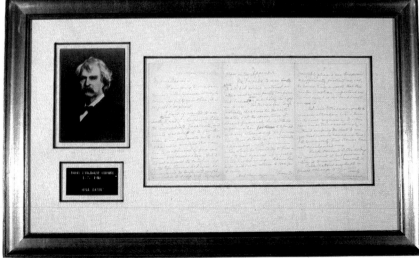

Autograph letter signed
by Horatio Alger, 1873.

Manuscript signed
by Carl Sandburg.

Manuscript signed
by Truman Capote.

Document signed by P.T. Barnum
(now in private collection).

Bank note
signed by
P.T. Barnum
(now in
private collection).

Autograph letter signed by
P.T. Barnum (now in private
collection).

1. Autograph note signed by Sarah Bernhardt, in French (now in private collection).
2. Signature of Lillie Langtry (now in private collection). 3. Rare signature of Will Rogers.
4. Typed letter signed by Harry Houdini.

Stock certificate signed by David O. Selznick.

Photograph signed by Cecil B. DeMille.

Signed photograph (unframed) of Charlie Chaplin.

Signature of Charlie Chaplin.

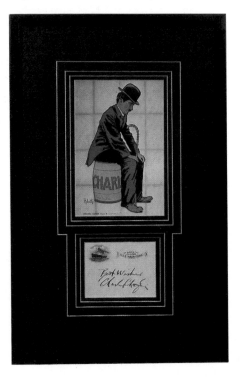

our legacy of freedom survived its infancy. The promissory note that I had purchased (dated March 27, 1782) represented the loan of $30,000 in silver to the government; thirty thousand dollars in silver coming from one individual—Haym Salomon! I was astounded at the magnitude of his risk and his patriotism. What kind of man would run such a risk with such an amount of money?

Born in Lissa, Poland in 1740, Salomon immigrated to America in 1772 and founded a mercantile and brokerage business in New York City. An avid patriot, Salomon was imprisoned by the British as a spy in 1776 and again in 1778 (when he was condemned to death), but escaped to American lines.

He moved to Philadelphia where he opened a brokerage business and became a prominent member of the small but highly influential Jewish community. In spite of the prejudices that existed in this country, the Jews in the United States felt that the new Republic offered them the same freedoms as it offered people of other faiths. This situation was so far removed from those in most of Europe that America must indeed have seemed like the "promised land." And the Philadelphia Jews were willing "to put their money where their mouths were." Haym Salomon alone contributed a total of $700,000—an amount equal to 35% of the Federal budget of $2,000,000.

Salomon became the Paymaster General of French forces in America and handled war subsidies advanced by the French and Dutch governments. Personally, he aided in maintaining American credit by extending large cash advances to the American treasury and by giving financial aid to many patriot leaders, including Jefferson and Madison.

But Salomon's story does not have the proverbial "happy ending." Although he had been an enormously successful man, Salomon began to feel the effects of the tuberculosis that he had contracted while imprisoned by the British, and on several occasions he attempted to recover some of the monies owed to him by the government—a government that somehow never had the money to repay him. Salomon succumbed to his illness in January of 1785. His wife was left penniless.

But the legacy of Haym Salomon was not over. The remarkable part of this story is that the note that I had acquired was not cancelled or marked paid. And the note, after research, was indeed found to be outstanding! Legal demand had been made on several occasions, initiated by Haym Salomon's son back in the early 1800's, and, although six Congressional committees had met and recommended payment, nothing had been done!

Chuckling at what this note for $30,000—even at the smallest rate of interest—would be worth today (at the end of 200 years), I made a few calculations—and found that the note could conceivably be worth $31,483,440,00 (as of September 27, 1983) if interest was compounded at 7% every 180 days! In addition to determining this staggering sum, I discovered that this note was a "bearer" instrument, meaning that the note was not made payable to Haym Salomon alone, but to the bearer—which is rather common in treasury instruments, even today.

But there is a legal dilemma. A Statute of Limitations that assigns a time after which rights cannot be enforced by legal action was passed by the Congress in 1911. However, this presents a very interesting legal problem since the note itself was written prior to any Statute of Limitations. The solution would be to get a bill passed that would prohibit the United States from using the Statute of Limitations as a defense for nonpayment.

I don't know what will happen in terms of payment for this obligation. However, if a successful attempt to gain payment is made, I would agree to place the proceeds (if permitted to do so by law) into a charitable foundation named in Haym Salomon's honor. My greatest accomplishment would be to gain national recognition for this great man and his important and courageous contributions to this country.

PROFILES IN HISTORY:
NAPOLEON BONAPARTE

Though there were countless French mothers who never forgave him for making cannon fodder of their sons, no name will stir deeper emotion in the hearts of patriotic Frenchmen than that of Napoleon Bonaparte. Napoleon was a charismatic opportunist, an egotistic pretender, and one of the most brilliant military commanders of all time. Few generals were as idolized and beloved by their troops as he was. Napoleon was often in the habit of snatching victory from a far superior foe,

Below: Photo of the The Three Stooges signed by Curly Joe. **Right:** Autograph note signed by Larry Fine of The Three Stooges.

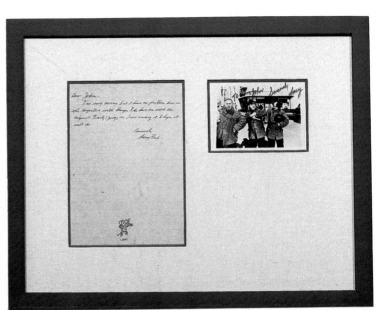

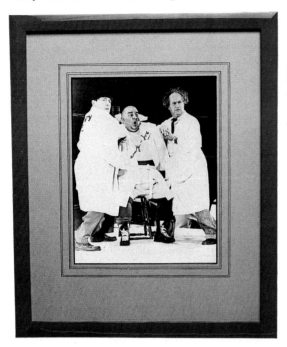

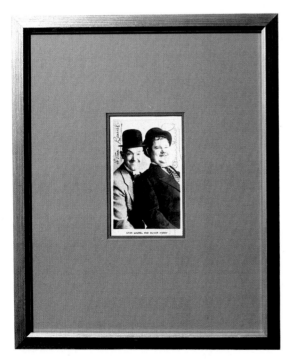

Above: Photo signed by Stan Laurel and Oliver Hardy (now in private collection). **Center, right:** Photo of The Marx Brothers signed by Groucho. **Bottom, right:** Application for the Friars Club signed by Groucho Marx.

130

Magazine cover autographed by W.C. Fields.

Autograph note signed by W.C. Fields (now in private collection).

Photo signed by Stepin Fetchit (now in private collection).

Application for Friars Club signed by Jack Benny.

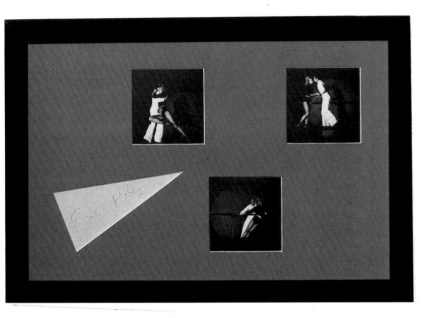

Signature of Gene Kelly.

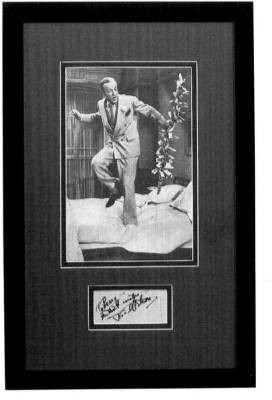

Photograph signed by Fred Astaire.

Vintage photo signed by Ginger Rogers.

Program and signature of James Cagney.

Signature of Maurice Chevalier
(now in private collection).

Signature of Liza Minelli.

Autograph note signed by Bing
Crosby (now in private collection).

Signature of Judy Garland (now
in private collection).

Signature of Barbra Streisand (now in
private collection).

There is every possibility that a collection that you assemble may well illuminate a new element of this tragic conflict.

THE ARTS: LITERATURE COMES ALIVE

If you happen to be a person who enjoys curling up in front of the fireplace with a good novel, collecting literary autographs and manuscripts can be a fulfilling and enjoyable activity. We cannot help but be intrigued by the lives and feelings of the men and women whose creativity has touched us so deeply.

Some writers, like Emily Dickinson and Marcel Proust, chose to create from a refuge of tranquility. Dickinson lived reclusively, quietly shaping fragile works of beauty; Proust, the ardent hypochondriac, sealed himself into a cork-lined room—where he eventually died. Other writers, such as Richard Henry Dana and Joseph Conrad, preferred the cauldron of human experience—transmuting flesh and blood into prose.

Writers whose work centered on political satire or protest often became a powerful force in their own right. Sometimes at great personal cost, these men and women became the speakers for a voiceless class or acted as the harbingers of change; Aleksandr Solzhenitsyn is a perfect example.

In learning about the travails and experiences of these writers, their successes and failures—written in their own hand—we can deepen our own understanding of the human experience. An author's letters and papers often precipitate the development of ideas and concepts that evolve into a powerful novel or play.

Very often, especially in the case of the major writers of any nation, the private collector must compete with institutions for available material. In American literature, Poe, Melville, Hawthorne, Emerson, and Thoreau are prime examples of authors beyond the reach of most private collectors. In spite of this fact, there are many authors not presently subject to the same vigorous collecting.

There are literally hundreds of significant authors who have contributed unforgettable works to the world's libraries and whose autographs are readily available. There are scores of English and American authors and playwrights whose autograph material is currently on the market. If you cannot build your collection around your favorite author, consider another author, perhaps one not quite so famous but of the same school or period.

While you might not be able to afford Walt Whitman or Emily Dickinson (and we can only guess at her reaction to the news that her rare letters sell in the thousands of dollars), you may be pleasantly surprised to discover who is within your reach. Oliver Wendell Holmes, Sr., Marianne Moore, Sinclair Lewis, and Theodore Dreiser are just a few examples of important American writers available at reasonable cost. And, very often, fine letters of writers like Longfellow and Thornton Wilder are available at a surprisingly low price.

Important collections can be built from a number of angles. For instance, if you have an interest in religion as well as literature, you might integrate these elements by collecting the material of novelists or playwrights who were heavily influenced by their religious beliefs (C.S. Lewis would be a case in point). Conversely, many of these novelists and playwrights have had a strong influence on the course of theological thought (consider Darwin's *Origin of Species* and the work of Thoreau).

Combining medicine and literature, one could collect the letters or journals of Sigmund Freud or Carl Jung. And Margaret Mead's letters, documents, and writings are extremely popular—especially in light of the recent controversy over her work.

Other collections might include journalists—such as Joseph Pulitzer, Edward R. Morrow, and Mark Twain (the most famous American author in the world); poets—such as Carl Sandburg, Robert Burns, and Edgar Allan Poe; humorists such as Ogden Nash, e.e. cummings, and Will Rogers. The great "Jazz Age" novelists—F. Scott Fitzgerald, Ernest Hemingway, and John Steinbeck—are popular; or you may wish to collect the papers of adventure writers James Fenimore Cooper, Robert Louis Stevenson, and Jack London.

THE ARTS: MUSIC HATH CHARMS

Great music, like great art, transcends the barrier of language. Music communicates the feelings and emotions that are common to all peoples. But until the turn of the century, musical autographs

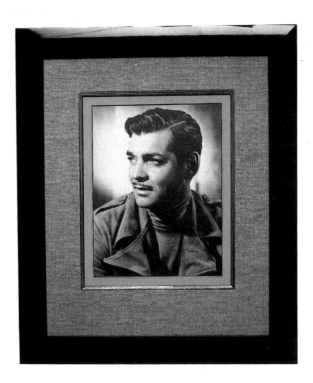

Above, left: Check signed by Clark Gable (now in private collection). **Above, right:** Vintage photo signed by Clark Gable.

Sketch signed by Carole Lombard.

Check signed by Clark Gable (now in private collection).

139

"lightweight" pursuit, I feel that this area deserves serious consideration—especially by the collector concerned with return on investment. Of greatest interest—and investment potential—are the stars with almost "cult" following: Marilyn Monroe, Judy Garland, Humphrey Bogart, Rudolph Valentino, and Jean Harlow (Harlow material is valuable for its rarity due to her short life span.)

Other stars worthy of serious consideration are John Wayne, Clark Gable, James Cagney, Carole Lombard, Mae West, and horror masters Boris Karloff and Bela Lugosi, or you may prefer those champions of justice, Superman (George Reeves) or the Lone Ranger (Clayton Moore).

Classic comedians are also an area expected to escalate in value. The materials of W.C. Fields, Charlie Chaplin, Laurel and Hardy, Groucho Marx, and The Three Stooges bring excellent returns.

THE SCIENCES: LABORATORIES NEED NOT BE BORING

Collecting scientific and medical autographs is often passed by in favor of pursuits that seem more "glamorous" at first glance. We tend to take for granted the scientific, technological, and medical advances that benefit our lives every day. We are inclined to think of the scientist as a bearded gentleman (apologies to Madame Curie) merrily boiling his concoctions—in happy isolation from the world around him. As with all stereotypes, nothing could be farther from the truth.

Sometimes forsaking comfortable lives and prestigious positions for the ridicule of their peers, scientists penetrated jungles and atoms in their search for truth. Their determined efforts have improved everyday human existence in countless ways. How many of us would risk livelihood and reputation for a cause adjudged lost by the foremost minds in the field?

Frequently persecuted by church, state, and even colleagues for their unorthodox beliefs, these men and women often extended the frontiers of human knowledge at great personal and professional cost. The battles of scientists and doctors throughout history, as documented in their letters, papers, and notes, enthrall the reader with their tireless struggle against disease, ignorance, and death.

But don't be fooled. Many scientists were really quite ordinary people characterized by a willingness to fail repeatedly then begin anew. Sheer genius played a lesser part than many of us suspect. As their letters and diaries show, the "noble seeker after the truth" was often a stubborn, irascible individual whose success came at the point of ultimate despair. Pressured by the responsibilities of family and lack of success, their advances frequently exacted a heavy personal toll.

Galileo, the immortal Italian physicist, astronomer, and mathematician, lived a precarious existence. What priceless autographs survive are beyond the reach of all but a very few institutions and private collectors. So too the works of Isaac Newton, the brilliant theoretician, and William Harvey, the English physician who laid the foundations of modern medicine with his discovery of the function of the heart and blood circulation.

Gregor Mendel, the geneticist; Edward Jenner, discoverer of a life saving vaccine for smallpox; Wilhelm Roentgen, father of X-rays; Alexander Fleming; Wilbur Wright; and Albert Einstein are just a few of the men whose autographs have continued to increase in value and decrease in availability.

When collecting medical or scientific autographs, two dilemmas arise. First, many of the autographs are written in the native language of the author. Many documents and papers are written in French, German, Italian, or even Latin, but this need not be a problem. Usually, a dealer will provide a description—if not a full translation—of the contents in his catalog. The original and the translation, framed either together or side by side, make for an interesting display.

The second problem area concerns the vast amount of material available. Letters of scientists concerning their fields of endeavor can be stimulating and informative, and, as mentioned, they are not always as esoteric as one might assume. Many well-known names are still available, and a collector exercising careful judgment can assemble a fine collection. If you are going to collect this type of autograph, I would suggest that you begin with a specific field of interest: surgeons, physicists, engineers, inventors, etc. Within those fields, you may wish to subdivide into categories such as atomic physics, or vaccines, or structural engineering.

★★

CHAPTER SUMMARY

As you can see, the world of historical documents is practically limitless, and collecting can take you on adventures that you never dreamed possible. Chapter VI will show you how collecting can develop into an exciting lifestyle or lucrative business from collections that were started as you are starting now (using the principles detailed in this book—and letting your imagination be the guide.)

Classic photo signed by Cary Grant.

Autograph note signed by Robert Taylor.

Signature of Errol Flynn (now in private collection).

Signature of Clark Gable (now in private collection).

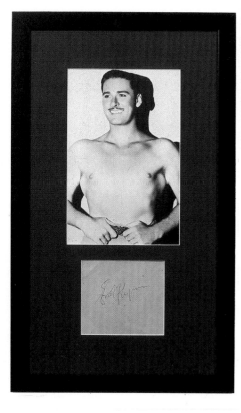

Photo signed by Robert Redford.

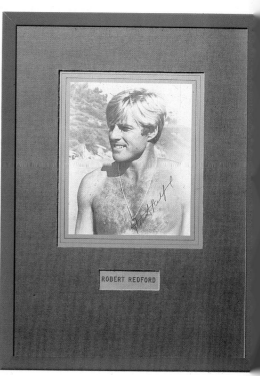

Left: Signature of John Wayne. **Above:** Document signed by John Payne (now in private collection).

Autograph letter signed by Ronald Reagan.

Autograph letter signed by Ronald Reagan (now in private collection).

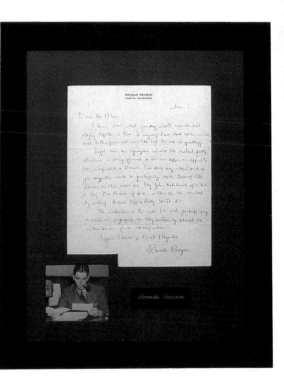

Chapter VI
Case Studies of Collectors—
How to Put It All Together

Once a collector has gained knowledge and expertise in the field of historical documents, there is no limit to the possibilities for personal involvement and satisfaction. This chapter will focus on several collectors who have used their imagination and taken that extra step into this exciting field. Included in this chapter is my personal experience—the acquisition of a collection that began with a single document and grew into the largest document dealership in the world.

THE MORGAN STORY

One of the most well-known collectors of historical documents was John Pierpont Morgan, the financier. The founder of the financial dynasty, Junius S. Morgan, had a modest collection of historical documents, and following his lead, his son J.P. Morgan (1837-1913) began his own collection with the letters of Methodist-Episcopal bishops, a collection that grew into the nucleus of the Morgan Library in New York City.

A believer in the adage "buy the best and you can never go wrong, buy the cheapest and you may lose," J.P. Morgan bought manuscripts at such high prices that many of his contemporaries warned that he would soon be bankrupt. (But good material in good condition never goes out of style, and today these manuscripts are worth fifty times as much as Morgan paid for them!)

J.P. Morgan collected with a vengeance—even to the extent of financing archeological expeditions to obtain ancient manuscripts—but his collection was a private affair. The library that he founded in New York City for the preservation of his materials was limited to the use of scholars and personal friends.

His collection was first publicly exhibited in January 1913 and left to the elder Morgan's son, J.P. Morgan (1867-1943), upon his death. The younger Morgan became actively involved in the activities of the library and continued in the acquisition of manuscripts. In 1924 (through George S. Hellman), Morgan bought a large part of the Stephen H. Wakeman collection—250 manuscripts by New England authors such as Nathaniel Hawthorne, Ralph Waldo Emerson, Henry Wadsworth Longfellow, Oliver Wendell Holmes, Sr., Edgar Allan Poe, and Henry David Thoreau—valued at $165,000.

In 1924, J.P. Morgan donated over 25,000 books, manuscripts, medals, artifacts, and other collectibles—and the building that housed them— to the City of New York. The Morgan Library is a legacy that continues to grow today, and in it can be found some of the world's greatest ancient documents.

THE EXPERIENCES OF
OTHER COLLECTORS

Although most collections will never reach the scope of the Morgan acquisitions, over the years collectors have found that collecting historical documents provides a positive influence in their lives. Some collectors have collected primarily for the joy of it (John F. Kennedy delighted in gathering important and interesting autograph letters); other collectors appreciate the decorative appeal of historical documents (a local collector has incorporated all the presidential signatures into his decor—his entry hall is a breathtaking example of history as art and is a constant source of beauty and inspiration to family and guests).

Collector involvement can lead to interesting and rewarding experiences as well. Some collectors have found that research into a particular document may involve them in remarkable adventures. This is evidenced by Carroll A. Wilson's fascinating story of his search for—and discovery of—two customhouse documents signed by

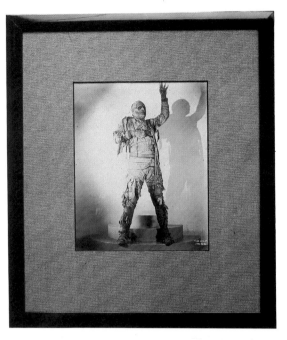

Photo signed
by Lon Chaney, Jr.

Signature of Charles Laughton.

Signature of Boris Karloff (now in private collection).

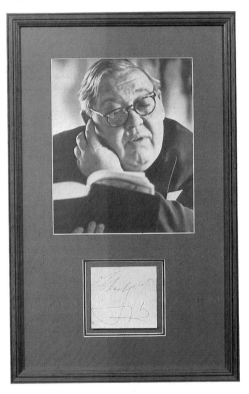

Photo signed
by Richard Burton.

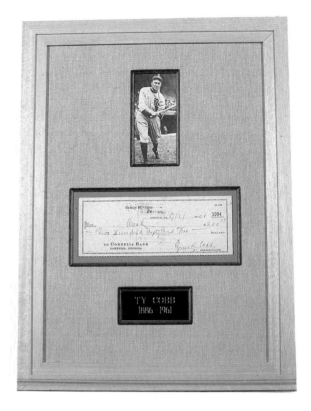

Above, upper photo: Classic photo signed by Jack Dempsey (now in private collection).
Lower photo: Signature of "Babe" Ruth and autograph letter signed by Claire Ruth.

Right, upper photo: Check signed by Ty Cobb. **Lower photo:** Signature and notes of Vince Lombardi; framed in a Green Bay jersey.

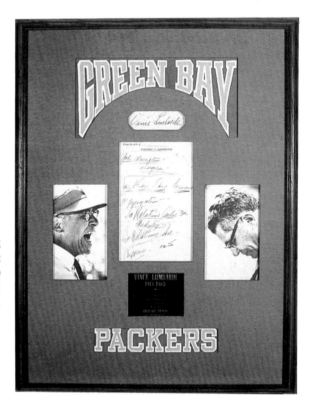

Nathaniel Hawthorne (used as source material for *The Scarlet Letter*) as recorded in his *Thirteen Author Collections*. My own experience with the Haym Salomon note (Chapter V) is another striking example of how a seemingly lifeless fragment of history can involve its owner in a modern-day detective story that breathes life into now-forgotten heroes.

Collectors with a personal interest in a subject have often become part of scholarly interest as a result of their hobby. Many—including myself—have found their collections to be of particular interest to universities and historical societies (in my own case, the University of California at Berkeley has made extensive use of the materials in my Mark Twain collection), and have had the satisfaction of knowing that we have made a contribution to the authentication of history.

Other collectors have become involved in community affairs as a result of their collections or have loaned manuscripts to libraries and museums for public viewing. My personal copy of the Thirteenth Amendment to the Constitution was the subject of much local interest when it was displayed at the University of Nevada at Las Vegas, and the exposure provided me with an opportunity to acquaint the general public with the world of historical documents.

Serious collectors have also been responsible for providing many of the documents in the world's greatest repositories and museums. The collection of William T. H. Howe (which included many pieces from the Stephen H. Wakeman collection of New England authors), formed a large part of the Berg Collection, now housed at the New York Public Library. Private manuscript libraries have also been founded by collectors. Henry E. Huntington, for example, began collecting in 1910 and spent millions of dollars on autographs and rare books; in 1920, he opened the Henry E. Huntington Library and Art Gallery in San Mateo, California. Other manuscript libraries have been founded by Thomas Addis Emmet, Ferdinand Dreer, Simon Gratz, Charles F. Gunther, and John Boyd Thacher.

MY PERSONAL EXPERIENCE

My own personal encounter with the world of historical documents began under rather inauspicious circumstances at New York University. Sitting in the office of a professor who was soundly chastising me for the lateness of a term paper, I was fascinated by a signed George Washington letter that was hanging on the wall over his desk.

Completely oblivious to everything else, I continued to stare at the letter. My exasperated professor, realizing that his words were having absolutely no effect on me, asked what was going on. I pointed to the framed document and asked (a question that I was later to hear repeated hundreds of times), "Is that real?"

The professor laughed, and the tone of our meeting changed; we spent the next three hours discussing historical documents. At the end of the discussion, I still had no idea how to actually go about collecting documents (the professor's small collection had been handed down through his family), but I had been bitten with the collecting bug.

My dream to own historical documents was put on hold as I finished my studies and began my career—first in real estate and later in the stock market and investment management. But the desire to collect always remained, and I was determined to learn more about collecting.

Several years after my introduction to the field of collecting, I met a lighting man from Hollywood who showed me a signed film script from the movie *David Copperfield*. Signed by all participants in the film—from the crew to the stars (including the autographs of Lionel Barrymore, W.C. Fields, Basil Rathbone, and David O. Selznick), this script became my first acquisition, and the excitement of this purchase prompted my contacting of MGM Studios—I wanted to create a suitable display setting for my find. For a modest fee, MGM provided contemporary prints from the original negatives of the film, and these stills, framed with the script, became a beautiful addition to my home. From that point on, there was no turning back. I was "hooked" on historical documents!

I contacted a couple of reputable dealers, and my collection grew. Not content to store these treasures away, I had them beautifully framed and proudly displayed my collection at my home and office. The clientele of my firm were just as enthusiastic about these pieces as I had been, and "Where'd you get it?", "How much does a piece like this cost?", and "I've just got to have it!" were some of the questions and comments I heard most often. Soon, friends and clients were literally buying my collection off the walls!

Encouraged by this reaction—and sensing a vast potential market for preserved, framed historical documents—I decided that it would be fun (and profitable) to open my own document dealership, an enterprise that would present historical documents in a setting that was fitting to their uniqueness. The concept of The American Museum of Historical Documents was born.

THE AMERICAN MUSEUM OF HISTORICAL DOCUMENTS

When I first considered founding The American Museum of Historical Documents, there were two motivating factors: my enjoyment of the field (quite simply, I thought that opening a dealership would be a nice thing to do) and my love of being involved. On a relative basis, I felt that historical documents were grossly undervalued, unique, one-of-a-kind collectibles, and I was determined to change this status. I realized that there was room for dramatic appreciation of historical documents (while still keeping autograph and manuscript material an exciting purchase within the financial reach of many), and I felt that increased public attention to this field would result in a dramatic escalation of values.

In creating the concept behind The American Museum of Historical Documents, I had several goals in mind:

1. To take historical documents "out of the closet" and promote them to their proper place in the world of collectibles.
2. To create exciting new ways of presenting and merchandising historical documents.
3. To preserve and protect the documents to museum specifications to ensure their safekeeping for generations to come.
4. To provide personalized service to collectors, satisfying the desire to collect and offering specialized, professional assistance.

I had no concrete idea as to how the Museum would do financially; after all, public awareness of the field of historical documents was limited (although there are 2,500 serious collectors and 10,000 casual collectors in the United States), and we would be presenting these documents in new and unusual ways. My only hope that first year was to break even.

I expanded my inventory base, investing $150,000 - $175,000 in pieces for the Museum (all of which were carefully preserved and handsomely displayed and framed). The Museum itself was established in The Fashion Show Mall (3200 Las Vegas Boulevard South, 530 The Fashion Show, Las Vegas, Nevada 89109), an exclusive "Strip" shopping center, and opened its doors in February 1982. The response was incredible, and that first year, The American Museum of Historical Documents was three times as successful as anticipated—with over $100,000 in sales the first month alone!

The phenomenal success of The American Museum of Historical Documents is understandable, however. One of the most important factors involved is our own satisfaction in promoting private ownership. Most history lovers visiting a traditional museum can view pieces but never hope to own them. The staff at The American Museum of Historical Documents finds great personal satisfaction in meeting with lovers of history and assuring them that they can indeed own these one-of-a-kind mementos of the past. We are fortunate enough to be able to make it possible for a collector to walk away with a personal treasure.

Selling historical documents is not unlike selling real estate. Clients looking for a home may state certain requirements (number of bedrooms, size of garage, location), but in most cases emotional considerations determine the sale (the weeping willow in the front yard, the winding staircase—a fitting backdrop for a daughter's first prom gown, the birds that remind one of a childhood home). Like real estate clients, the purchasers of historical documents are almost always emotionally involved with their fragment of history; decorative appeal and investment values figure far behind—serving only to "back up" the purchase.

The staff at The American Museum of Historical Documents also feels a personal involvement with the documents offered for sale and will not knowingly sell to anyone who does not have a respect for the value of historical documents. We have been privileged to acquire the three most important Abraham Lincoln documents in existence today: Lincoln's personal copy of the Thirteenth Amendment, a signed copy of the Emancipation Proclamation, and Lincoln's reply to Grace Bedell. It was the first time in history that all three pieces were united in one place under a single ownership. On September 10, 1983, a West Coast real estate developer pur-

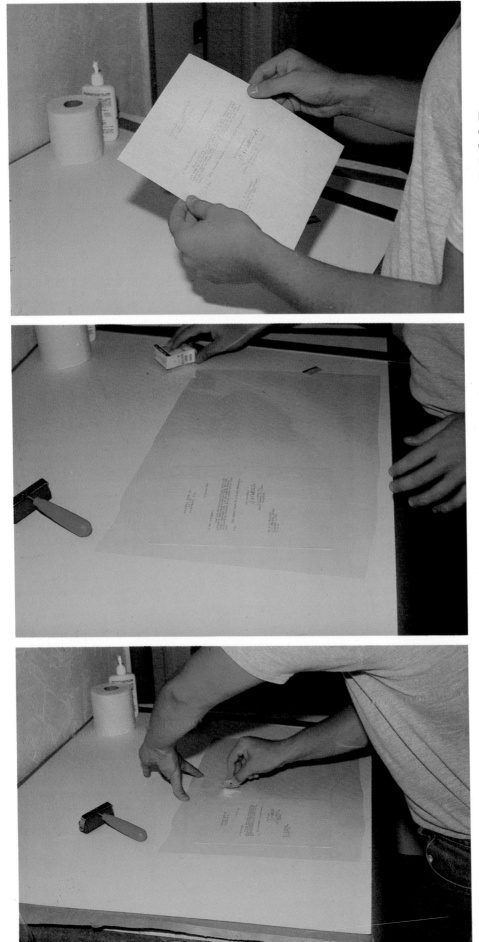

Pieces are carefully checked for existing damage. In some cases, restoration will be recommended.

Acid-free Mylar is placed under document to begin encapsulation process.

Mylar is trimmed to slightly larger than document size.

In these three photographs, double-sided, non-acidic polyester transparent tape is used to affix the document to the Mylar.

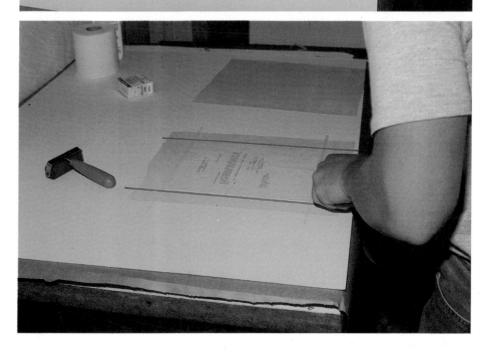

chased the Thirteenth Amendment and the Emancipation Proclamation, promising that these two pieces would never again be separated. The "Lincoln Triad" may never be found in one place again, but the owner of the remaining two documents will treasure his invaluable milestones in history.

This care and respect is of utmost importance to our staff. On one occasion, I refused to sell a letter of Anwar Sadat to a wealthy Arab whose intention was to purchase the document to relegate it to one of the back rooms of his mansion. I felt that this letter—a beautifully written, almost poetic, insight into this great leader—deserved far more respectful treatment and was determined that it would be sold only to an owner who could appreciate its great significance and beauty.

Our commitment to elevating historical documents to their rightful place in the world of collectibles is also evident in the quality of the pieces presented. While there are other outlets that sell framed pieces, I saw that this was an area in which quality was lacking (in many cases, pieces were preserved but cheaply framed); it was my intention to take this old collecting idea and present documents as new, fine art that could be proudly displayed.

To achieve this goal, I developed a formula that results in the creation of a museum quality finished product: a document preserved with care and beauty, a unique piece that any collector would be proud to own. Ninety percent of this formula consists of factors that are not readily apparent—restoring and preserving the document to museum specifications; the other ten percent of the formula is to create an esthetically attractive and self-explanatory setting for the document.

In accomplishing these goals of first-class restoration and presentation, the following steps are taken:

1. *Restoration.* The condition of a document is of utmost importance, and if the condition is unacceptable (due to existing damage such as "foxing," water spots, or tears), we seek out the top two or three restorers in the country to de-acidify the document.

2. *Encapsulation.* Documents in our inventory are encapsulated before being stored for proper preservation before framing. Documents are sealed at all four edges bet-

ween two pieces of acid-free Mylar (bonded together using acid-free adhesive backings—polyester transparent tape—according to Library of Congress standards) that form a protective envelope.

3. *Design.* Balance is the prime consideration in document display, and careful planning determines the use of photographs (or engravings), brass plates (describing the person, document, or both), mattings and frames that will enhance the beauty of the document. Only premium materials—leather, suede, silk, linen—are used for mattings. (We could use cheaper mattings and many customers wouldn't know the difference—but *we* would; we use the same standards for our customers as we would for our personal pieces, and our customers appreciate the difference.)

Moldings are also of the highest quality materials used in the market today. Exotic hardwoods (padouk, bubinga, koa), oak, teak, mahogany, and the top grade of gold and silver leaf is used in framing. Even seemingly ordinary frames get special treatment—a simple wooden frame may receive up to 42 coats of lacquer!

4. *Display Preparation.* The next step involves cutting out the matting pieces (and their coverings) and fillets (inner mats to the fabric to accentuate the document or wooden inserts to match the frame) and placing the pieces to view the result.

5. *Document Installation.* The document is put in place using museum-quality materials to ensure lasting protection of the document. The entire mat and any fillets in the inner mat are backed by 100% rag museum board, as is the document (when the document is affixed to the mat, archival quality adhesives are used). Once the document is put in place, a double thickness of 100% rag museum board is placed around the document for its further protection. Plates and photographs are also affixed to museum specifications, assuring an acid-free environment.

6. *Finishing.* Lastly, UF-3 Plexiglas (scientifically designed to inhibit ultra-violet rays and thus prevent documents from fading) is cut and the display is fitted into the frame. The display is dust-sealed, and hangers are applied to complete the work.

These steps create a finished piece that is exciting and esthetically beautiful, but this beauty is more than skin deep. Although special handling involves additional expense (the most inexpensive framing process averages $250.00), this first-class treatment has greatly enhanced the collecting appeal of historical documents. It is our feeling that these documents are museum pieces worthy of the cost of this care.

The Museum also offers other quality personalized services. Instead of a generic catalog, a "wants list" is maintained for individuals interested in a specific person, subject, or type of material. The staff is trained in document search and will investigate auctions, estate sales, and the establishments of other reputable dealers to locate authentic signed pieces for collectors.

All documents are fully guaranteed and a certificate of authenticity accompanies each purchase. This practice—and its commitment to customer satisfaction—has made The American Museum of Historical Documents one of the 25 most respected document dealers in the world.

Plans now call for the establishment of museums in major cities across the country (the first branch is scheduled to open in December 1983 in Dallas). And The American Museum of Historical Documents will "go public" in the Spring/Summer of 1984, affording investors the opportunity of taking advantage of the coming boom in document sales.

★★★

CHAPTER SUMMARY

While your own collection may not reach the proportions of mine, collecting historical documents will nonetheless prove a rewarding experience. By following the guidelines outlined in this book, your collection will provide personal and financial benefits and satisfaction and bring years of pleasure and enjoyment.

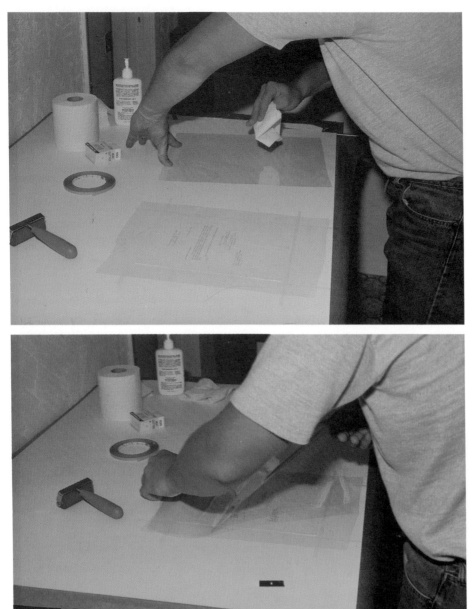

Document is completely affixed to first sheet of Mylar.

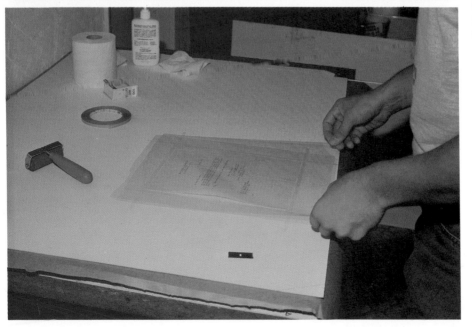

In these two photographs, a second sheet of Mylar is placed over the document and properly positioned.

Using a brayer, the two sheets are sealed; forming a protective envelope for the document.

The Mylar is trimmed to complete the encapsulation process.

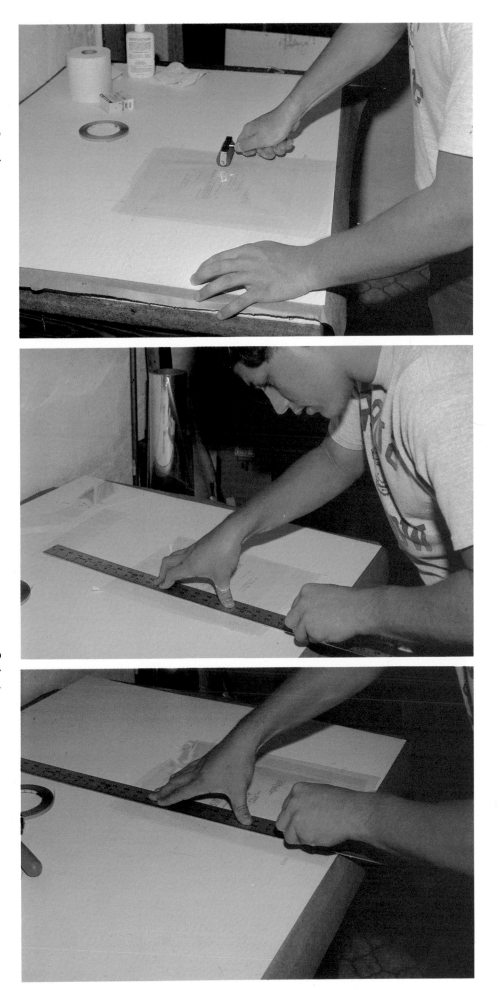

Chapter VII
Projected Growth Curve

One of the biggest problems in describing any market (especially one that is low priced and undervalued at the start) that is about to enter a dynamic growth phase is that percentages can be overwhelming and, therefore, not believable. A 1000% appreciation boggles the imagination, and yet it is very easy (and believable) for an item to go from $100 to $1,000—much easier than for an item to go from $100,000 to $1,000,000. Yet the percentages are the same; it's just the numbers that scare most people away.

A LeRoy Neiman lithograph (a facsimile of the artist's original work) can sell for between $5,000 and $7,000, while an entry level Abraham Lincoln document, signed as President, may sell for one-third of that price. Should the Lincoln document appreciate to a parity with the Neiman lithograph, the document would have appreciated over 300% (yet in terms of dollars, the price would have gone from $2,000 to $6,000).

When a Ronald Reagan letter written prior to his Presidency (as an old-time movie star) would sell for $50, at $750 it is selling for fifteen times its price value prior to Reagan's Presidency (in real terms it has only appreciated $700). So it is very important that we shy away from percentages because they can be so overwhelming as to create a credibility problem. The important concept is an overall appraisal of the current price levels of investment-grade autograph and manuscript material—and their projected values twenty years from now.

Unlike gold, silver, and diamonds (which have historically been used as standards of value by tangible property collectors), investment-grade autograph and manuscript material, especially that of deceased personages, has a diminishing supply. There is more gold in existence today than there was yesterday, and there will be more tomorrow than there is today. We don't have that luxury when it comes to the investment-grade

autograph and manuscript material of a deceased author.

Since dealers and collectors can purchase only what is available for sale in the private sector, we are looking at a diminishing supply of material. For example, there was a finite amount of material signed by Abraham Lincoln during his lifetime. Since his death, large quantities of these materials have been institutionalized. Further, natural causes such as floods, fires, and deterioration have claimed a tremendous number of these documents, so that each year we see fewer and fewer original Lincoln documents and letters in private hands.

Therefore, a basic economic analysis of the laws of supply and demand reveals a diminishing supply and a dramatically increasing demand. Simple projection of this in economic terms places price levels impressively higher, and I believe that an arithmetic increase in the number of collectors will, over time, produce a geometric increase in price levels.

In terms of relative value, I believe that twenty years from now we will be able to look back at the 1984 price levels and remark at how cheap they really were in comparative terms. It is my belief that we will look back on today's prices in investment-grade autograph and manuscript material in the same way that past generations looked back at the prices of new automobiles of the 1920's era ("I remember when you could buy a . . .").

If you are one of the many readers who have had no previous exposure to autograph and manuscript material, you can base some of your own conclusions on comparing price levels with those of other collectibles with which you are familiar—such as art, lithographs, and other similar collectibles. The fact that you can still buy an Abraham Lincoln letter for under $5,000 or a George Washington letter for under $7,500 should compare favorably with any other analysis

Balance is important in designing the display, and pieces are carefully assembled and arranged for an aesthetically pleasing yet self-explanatory finished work.

Once the design has been created, a layout is drawn and pieces set in tentative positions to view effect.

Corresponding pieces are cut from the approved layout.

done with existing collectibles of unique, one-of-a-kind materials. For that matter, the comparison should be very favorable even with non-unique and eclectic items.

It is for these reasons that I have invested millions of dollars (many millions of dollars) in these materials and have dedicated my life to the collection and preservation of investment-grade autograph and manuscript materials and to the education of the population with regard to the opportunities of owning these remarkable collectibles.

There are a number of areas of collecting which have a high growth and return potential. Investments in materials of the individuals in the following categories are expected to show the greatest appreciation over the next decade.

ART

John James Audubon	Frederic Remington
Marc Chagall	Pierre August Renoir
Henri Emile Matisse	Peter Paul Rubens
Grandma Moses	Charles Marion Russell
Pablo Picasso	Rembrandt van Rijn

AVIATION

Participants in the U.S. Space Program (especially the original seven astronauts, Gemini, and Apollo crews).

Amelia Earhart	Wilbur and
Charles Lindbergh	Orville Wright
Billy Mitchell	

BUSINESS AND FINANCE

John Jacob Astor	J. Paul Getty
Phineas Taylor	Jay Gould
(P.T.) Barnum	H. L. Hunt
Bernard Baruch	J. P. Morgan
Andrew Carnegie	John D. Rockefeller
Jay Cooke	William "Boss" Tweed
William Fargo	Cornelius Vanderbilt
Henry Ford	Henry Wells

ENTERTAINMENT

Humphrey Bogart	Greta Garbo
James Cagney	Judy Garland
Lon Chaney, Sr.	Jean Harlow
Charlie Chaplin	Boris Karloff
Walt Disney	Laurel and Hardy
W.C. Fields	Carole Lombard
Clark Gable	Bela Lugosi

Marx Brothers (group photos)	Rudolph Valentino
	John Wayne
Marilyn Monroe	Mae West
The Original Three Stooges (group photo)	

HISTORY

Signers of the Declaration of Independence

Aaron Burr	Marquis de Lafayette
Winston Churchill	Paul Revere
Benjamin Franklin	Haym Salomon
John Hancock	

INVENTORS

Alexander Graham Bell	Guglielmo Marconi
Samuel Colt	Samuel F. B. Morse
Thomas Alva Edison	James Watt
Robert Fulton	

LAW

Pieces on which all signatures of Associate Justices and Chief Justices appear on the same document.

Henry Clay	J. Edgar Hoover
Clarence Darrow	John Jay
Alexander Hamilton	John Marshall
Oliver Wendell Holmes, Jr.	Roger B. Taney

LITERATURE

Edgar Allan Poe	Margaret Mitchell
Charles Dickens	Carl Sandburg
Ralph Waldo Emerson	Percy B. Shelley
Ernest Hemingway	John Steinbeck
John Keats	Henry David Thoreau
Rudyard Kipling	Mark Twain
Herman Melville	Walt Whitman

MEDICINE

Sir Frederick Banting	Joseph Lister
Clara Barton	The Mayo Brothers
Sigmund Freud	Florence Nightingale
Edward Jenner	Sir William Osler
Carl Jung	Albert Schweitzer

MILITARY

Confederate Civil War materials.

Antonio Santa Anna	Jefferson Davis
Stephen Austin	Karl Doenitz
Pierre G.T. Beauregard	Dwight D. Eisenhower
Napoleon Bonaparte	David Farragut

John C. Fremont
Ulysses S. Grant
Adolf Hitler
Samuel Houston
John Paul Jones
Robert E. Lee
George Meade

Montgomery of Alamein
Horatio Nelson
George C. Patton
John Pershing
George Pickett
Winfield Scott
Zachary Taylor

MUSIC

Johann S. Bach
Ludwig van Beethoven
Johannes Brahms
Franz Liszt
Felix Mendelssohn
Niccolo Paganini
Giacomo Puccini

Sergei Rachmaninoff
Maurice Ravel
Gioacchino Rossini
Samuel Francis Smith
John Philip Sousa
Richard Wagner

PRESIDENTS

NOTE: While most Presidential documents (especially those written during the Presidency dates) can be expected to steadily appreciate in value, investment in the materials of the following Presidential figures will offer the greatest potential return:

John Adams
James Garfield
William Henry Harrison
Thomas Jefferson
Andrew Johnson
Lyndon B. Johnson
John F. Kennedy

Abraham Lincoln
James Madison
Richard Nixon
James K. Polk
Theodore Roosevelt
Zachary Taylor
George Washington

SCIENCE

Madame Marie Curie
Charles Darwin
Albert Einstein
Michael Faraday

Joseph Henry
Sir Isaac Newton
Louis Pasteur
Nikola Tesla

SPORTS

Abner Doubleday
Lou Gehrig
Vince Lombardi
Jesse Owens

Knute Rockne
George "Babe" Ruth
Jim Thorpe

WESTERN

William "Billy the
  Kid" Bonney
W.F. "Buffalo Bill"
  Cody
Henry Derringer
Wyatt Earp
Pat Garrett
Richard Gatling

Geronimo
J.W. Hardin
James "Wild Bill"
  Hickok
Jesse James
William "Bat"
  Masterson
Sitting Bull

Beautifully framed pieces from each of these areas are available for immediate sale at The American Museum of Historical Documents. In addition, our capable staff can provide full-service collection and investment planning to enable you to take full advantage of this exciting market!

Matting material is wrapped around museum board in preparation for creating display area.

Any needed fillets are placed inside the lining of the matting material.

The matting is cut according to the display layout.

Oval and circle cutter used to cut and shape display pieces.

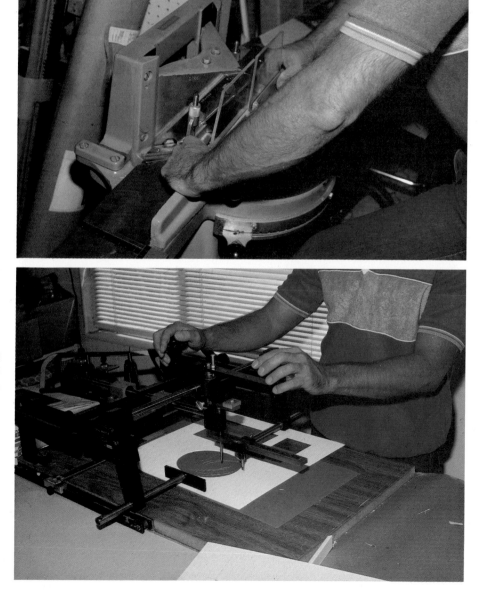

Shaping the matting pieces from patterns on layout.

Appendix A
The Development of Papers, Inks, and Pens

All collectors of autographs and manuscripts should possess a passing familiarity with papers, pens, and inks. Expertise in these areas is not a prerequisite for collecting, but a knowledge of the basics will acquaint you with some of the problems associated with the storage and preservation of fine holographic material. An understanding of the "tools of the trade" will enable you to comprehend some of the techniques used by experts to unmask forgeries. Additionally, the development of our present day writing materials was a gradual evolutionary process of great interest to most collectors.

PAPERS

Traditionally, the development of writing materials began five thousand years ago, when Menes, King of Upper Egypt, subjugated the Nile Delta. His victories unified Egypt for the first time, initiating the rule of the First Dynasty. During this period we see the first use of papyrus, the ancestor of modern-day paper.

Though rare today, the papyrus plant grew abundantly in ancient Egypt. This simple sedge was a source of heat, light, clothing, and power. (In its multiplicity of uses, it provided the Egyptian people with many of the same benefits provided to the American Indians by the great bison.) The Egyptians derived fuel from the dried roots of the papyrus and food from its pith, and vital necessities like sails, sandals, and rope were woven, pounded, or matted from its tough ropy stem. Even the "bulrushes" that hid Moses from Pharaoh's executioners were most likely papyrus plants.

The papyrus paper that we commonly refer to today was a series of small, handmade sheets approximately five or six inches wide and eight or nine inches long. Too cumbersome and brittle to be folded, the sheets were glued end-to-end and rolled around wooden batons to form a scroll.

The manufacturing process of papyrus involved placing a horizontal layer of strips or pith over a vertical layer of strips or pith. The sliced pith was then pressed with a primitive glue (probably made by combining plant sap with water) and allowed to dry in the sun. Fully dried, the papyrus was scraped with a shell or similar instrument to smooth out the surface. Finally, the individual sheets were glued together to form a scroll. And the papyrus plant even provided the pen—a cut reed.

Papyrus was adopted by the Greeks and Romans for their own benefit and was in continuous use until it was gradually replaced by parchment and vellum, innovations introduced around 300 B.C. During that historical period, the Macedonian Empire, created by Alexander the Great, was slowly disintegrating, but its cultural remains provided a rich humus for the civilizations that rose in its wake. Pergamum was the seat of one such civilization.

A center of culture and learning, Pergamum was located in modern day Turkey, and its inhabitants were famed for their sculpture, superb examples of which exist today. The rulers of Pergamum were also renowned for their impressive library—which was second only to the great library at Alexandria.

Credit for the development of parchment is generally given to Eumenes II, ruler of Pergamum from 197 B.C. to 160 B.C. The process that Eumenes II developed represented a major innovation in the evolution of writing material. Untanned animal hides (most often sheep, goat, or calf) were soaked, and hair was removed by the application of lime. The skins were scraped, stretched, and dried. Powdered chalk was sprinkled onto the parchment to whiten it, and the surface was rubbed with pumice to produce a smooth finish. Parchment proved to be more durable than papyrus—and easier to use.

Perhaps its greatest advantage was its flexibility; unlike papyrus, parchment could be folded, eliminating the need for the cumbersome rollers. Exceptionally high grade parchment, made from calfskin or kid, came to be known as vellum. (Vellum was used throughout the Middle Ages, until it was replaced by paper.)

Like gunpowder and so many other ingenious inventions, paper came to us from the Chinese. Ts'ai Lun is credited with processing the first paper in 105 A.D. Jealously guarded by the Chinese, the secret was kept for 650 years until 751 A.D. when the Chinese suffered defeat at the hands of the Arabs at Samarkand. Captured Chinese papermakers were forced to divulge their secrets, and the first papermill was built in Samarkand that very same year. Four hundred years later, the first mill was built in Europe (in Toledo, Spain), and mills spread throughout Europe over the succeeding 450 years. The first mill in America was built in Germantown, Pennsylvania in 1690.

Bark and hemp were the original materials used by the Chinese as a source of fibers for papermaking. The Europeans used flax and hemp prior to the discovery that rags are the best source of fibers. Interestingly enough, today's finest papers are still made from rag fibers.

To make paper, the source material (be it rags, flax and hemp, or any other fibrous substance) is soaked in water. Continuous soaking breaks down the base material into a fibrous pulp. This pulp is then beaten to separate the fibers, and more water is added to form a suspension. At this stage the papermaker dips a mold into the liquefied pulp, coming up with a layer of fibers.

This point in the process is one of particular interest to collectors of autographs. In the early stages of paper production, the Chinese used a mold constructed of fine reeds. These reeds left minute furrows in the paper, uniquely identifying the mold. As technology improved, wires were substituted for reeds. And as the manufacture of wire became more sophisticated, thinner gauges became available to the papermaker.

Eventually, during the 1700's, papermakers discovered that optimum results could be obtained using wires woven through the cloth. The layer of fibers was then deposited on a piece of felt. The felt and fiber leaves were then piled on top of one another and pressed to remove the moisture. Once this was accomplished, the paper was hung over ropes to air dry. The final step consisted of dipping the paper into a gelatin solution, drying it, and rubbing the surface with a smooth stone. This created a smooth, level surface for writing.

Of importance to the autograph collector are the indelible markings left on the paper by the molding process. These marks are called "chain lines." The wires that formed the mold were, and still are, referred to as "laid wires." Paper made by this process is called "laid paper," and encompasses all paper made in Europe until the cloth-wire mold was developed in the eighteenth century. "Wove paper" takes its name from the woven wire which was subsequently developed and used in molds. This type of mold left a characteristic grid of equi-spaced lines running both horizontally and vertically.

Another matter of interest to the autograph collector is the "watermark." Beginning in 1825, papermakers began to weave a personal trademark into the mold. The translucent impression left on the paper by this trademark was clearly visible when the paper was held up to a light and was known as a "watermark."

Perhaps the greatest innovation in paper manufacture was the Fourdrinier machine. A Frenchman by the name of Nicholas Robert invented a machine that would manufacture paper; and, although it did need some work, Robert was confident. His confidence was not shared by his countrymen, but undeterred by his lack of success in France, Robert did what few Frenchmen would do, even today—he crossed the Channel to England, where the Fourdrinier brothers were delighted to be of service.

The two brothers hired Brian Conklin, a brilliant engineer, who retooled the machine, and successful paper production began in 1803. The paper manufactured through this process was devoid of laid lines and watermarks until 1826 when the 'dandy roll' was added to the machine. This innovation made it possible to impress a watermark and laid lines on the paper before it was rolled. In spite of this clever addition to the manufacturing process, it is still possible to distinguish the difference between Fourdrinier's paper and genuine wove paper. Wove wire lines are visible on the back side on the paper (under magnification) while the Fourdrinier process left marks only on the front surface—lines did not penetrate through to the opposite side.

Display pieces are affixed (hinged) to 100% rag museum board using archival quality adhesives.

Matting is affixed to document board.

Frame is fitted around display area.

UF-3 Plexiglas, designed to inhibit ultra-violet rays and thus prevent documents from fading, is cut to fit frame.

Fitted UF-3 Plexiglas is placed over finished display.

Document unit is affixed to frame.

One additional factor is helpful in determining paper age. Until 1807, paper was sized with gelatin, creating a smooth surface. In 1807, Morris Illig discovered that adding rosin to the pulp mash eliminated the need for gelatin sizing. As the paper was rolled over a heated drum, the rosin melted and sized the paper automatically. It is very easy to differentiate between the two types of sizing.

Armed with this simple information, the collector of autographs and manuscripts is capable of protecting himself against the most blatant of forgeries. A letter written by Napoleon Bonaparte on woodpulp stationery (woodpulp was not used as a source of fibers until the early 1860's) is an obvious fake, gilt-edged or not.

For those collectors interested in a detailed study of paper and its development, the following books are available: *Watermarks, Mainly of the 17th and 18th Centuries,* Edward Heawood, 1950; *Old Papermaking,* Dard Hunter, 1923; *Papermaking: The History and Technique of an Ancient Craft,* Dard Hunter, 1943; *Papermaking by Hand in America,* Dard Hunter, 1950; *Dictionary and Encyclopedia of Paper and Papermaking,* E.J. Labarre, 1952; *The Nature and Making of Parchment,* Ronald Reed, 1976; *Paper Mills and Paper Makers in England, 1495-1800,* Alfred H. Shorter, 1957; *Paper as Bibliographical Evidence,* Allan Henry Stevenson, 1962; and *A History of Paper Manufacturing in the United States, 1690-1916,* Lyman Horace Weeks, 1916.

INKS

Throughout recorded history, in his search for ways to record his study for future generations, mankind has experimented with all types of writing fluids and compounds, seeking clarity, permanence, and ease of use. Primitive inks were manufactured from dyes made with tree barks or berries. Even blood was given a trial, but its clotting qualities hardly made for smooth, even flow or storage, to say nothing of the flies that an exposed bottle tended to attract. Sepia from squid, octopus, and cuttlefish was also used as ink by early peoples, but most of these inks were difficult to store, hard to use, and far from permanent.

Once again, the Chinese take credit for another ingenious innovation. "India" or "China" ink was made from water, carbon black, and gum. It was everything its predecessors were not: easily stored and convenient to use, this permanent black ink is still used in China and Japan today (and is prized by engineers, artists, and draftsmen for its color and indelibility).

"Lampblack" was a similar ink developed by the Arabs. Composed of oil-tar soot, gum, and honey, lampblack was manufactured as small cakes to which water would be added to create ink.

The ink that concerns most autograph collectors of today is iron gall ink. Midnight black when first used, it fades to a rusty brown due to the evaporation of the water in the ink, but this ink is very similar to the black and blue-black ink of today.

Although this type of ink is made today from refined chemicals and preservatives, it is interesting to note that the original iron gall ink, first used perhaps as early as the second century, owes its existence to the female gall wasp. Her sting produces an abnormal swelling or "gall" on oak trees and certain other varieties of vegetation. When dried and powdered, these "gall nuts" were mixed with certain iron salts to produce a durable black ink. (Without doubt, the first man to discover this unlikely combination of materials must have possessed the same tenacity and courage as the first man to eat an oyster!)

The chemical composition of iron gall is of prime importance to collectors. Gallic and tannic acids are present in the ink, making it highly corrosive. Over the long term, the destructive capabilities of these acids are impressive; given enough time and the proper conditions (especially excessive humidity), the ink can eat right through the paper. This process can be arrested through deacidification, a technique discussed in Chapter IV.

Iron gall ink came into common usage in the eleventh century and remained unchallenged until the invention of aniline inks in the 1860's. Aniline inks were water-soluble and consisted of the blue dye obtained from the indigo plant; modern manufacturers use a benzene derivative.

For additional information on inks, the following books will prove helpful: *Forty Centuries of Ink, or a Chronological Narrative Concerning Ink and Its Background,* David N. Carvalho, 1904; *Inks, Their Composition and Manufacture,* Charles Ainsworth Mitchel, 1937; and *Inks,* C. E. Waters, U.S. Government Printing Office, 1940.

PENS

An extensive study of pens would occupy an entire volume, and collectors interested in pursuing the subject should avail themselves of a more comprehensive text. But the brief history that follows will provide an introduction into this fascinating area.

Our early ancestors probably used sharpened sticks to draw or write in the dirt. Most likely, a more sophisticated version of this wooden "pen" was used to inscribe clay tablets, such as the stylus made of a sharpened reed used by the ancient Egyptians.

Though primitive metal pens have been found in the ruins of Pompeii, the reed pen was the predominate writing instrument until the seventh century. During that time the goosequill came into use, and this method of writing remained unchallenged for more than a millenium.

The first steel pens made their appearance in the late eighteenth century, but their stiff qualities and high cost restricted their widespread use. Soon after the turn of the century, manufacturing techniques were improved, resulting in a flexible, inexpensive steel nib that replaced the goosequill.

The next major advance occurred in 1884, when L. E. Waterman patented the first fountain pen. For the first time, a writing instrument with a large, self-contained reservoir of ink was available. Needless to say, its use spread like wildfire.

Ballpoint pens are probably our most common present day writing instrument. It is interesting to note that a patent was filed for a ballpoint pen in the same year that Waterman patented his fountain pen, but it was not until the late 1930's that a workable ballpoint was manufactured. Even then, the pen failed to catch on until it was officially adopted for use by the United States Army in 1944. The rest, of course, is history.

In these three photos, black craft paper is fitted to the back of the piece, dust-sealing the finished display.

Black craft paper is
trimmed to size.

Black craft paper backing
material is affixed to completed framed piece.

Appendix B
A History of Communications and Collecting

THE ART OF COMMUNICATION

Nearly 20,000 years ago, man began to paint and carve images of his world onto the walls of caves. Some of these "autographs" of early man survive today, reaching across the millenia to touch us with their grace and depth of simplicity. These drawings convey a message that transcends time, leaving us to wonder about the man whose hand created those works of art, wishing we could know more about his hopes, his dreams, his fears.

We can only imagine man's need to communicate more than just a reflection of the powerful creatures that provided him with clothing and food: his desire to record and preserve the glory of a hunt that would be remembered for generations. And man did begin to expand his vision, illustrating an event rather than a single image—carving or painting an entire sequence of events.

Having no written language, Cro-Magnon man sought to improve his artistic abilities to preserve a "written" record of his life. Cave dwellings in Altimira, in Northern Spain, and in the neighboring Dordogne valley of Southern France, display Paleolithic art at its zenith. Figures were sketched in charcoal or pigments and the creators of these works demonstrated a relatively keen sense of perspective. The broken, uneven contours of the cave walls were cleverly decorated to impart a three-dimensional air. Images were skillfully shaded with a variety of colors, applied with fingers, sticks, primitive moss "brushes," or hollow bones through which pigments were blown.

These images testify to man's basic need to reach beyond himself. They are a remarkable achievement for a race noted for its short life span and constant struggle to survive. As the accumulated knowledge of each generation was passed to the next, these pictographic narratives communicated a basic message that we have no trouble understanding ten or twenty thousand years

later. These drawings deal with the most common denominators of human existence—the awareness of powers more awesome than ourselves, the need for food and shelter, the desire to share our experiences with others of our kind, and the need to leave something of ourselves that will reach beyond our own short lives.

Three thousand years before the birth of Christ, a great civilization arose between the Tigris and Euphrates Rivers in ancient Mesopotamia. The founders of this civilization are known to us as the Sumerians. Their educated priesthood evolved a phonetic system of writing based on "sounds" rather than "pictures." Originally, the Sumerians used a purely pictographic system, then evolved to a hybrid form of pictographic symbols that were used to represent phonetic sounds. We call this writing "cuneiform," meaning "wedge-shaped."

The Sumerians kept their records on wet clay tablets, using a stylus as a writing instrument. When completed, the tablets were fired and stored in "libraries"—many of which have been excavated by archeological teams. As we study these records today, we come away with a graphic image of civilized life in ancient Mesopotamia.

About the same time another great civilization arose in Egypt, chronicling its culture and history in hieroglyphics. Like the Sumerians, the Egyptians began with pictograms and evolved to the use of phonetics. In many ancient civilizations that took root in the eastern Mediterranean and Near East, pictographic writing evolved to a system employing phonetic sounds. In other words, a picture or pictogram was no longer simply representative of just an image—it could also represent a sound. The next major step was the development of a phonetic alphabet.

As man's civilization began to flourish, heavy demands were made for accurate tallies, inventories of trade goods, and financial accountings.

Development of a phonetic alphabet most likely occurred in the area currently occupied by present-day Israel and Syria. This region was crisscrossed by merchants and traders seeking markets for their goods and new merchandise for consumers at home. The new phonetic alphabet drew on the linguistic resources of many countries; the end result was a written script in which one symbol or character corresponded to a single sound.

Another factor contributing to the rise of a phonetic alphabet was the inherent difficulty of pictographic writing; it required an enormous amount of painstaking labor to create the images. The increasing need for written records generated by the creation of an empire and ever-expanding trade required a quicker, more efficient method of recording information. In the case of the Egyptians, the demands of the empire were met by the evolution of the hieratic, then demotic script—each being more convenient to use than its predecessor. This evolutionary process was repeated again and again, continuously borrowing, abridging, and creating to facilitate the recording of information.

In the case of the English language, centuries of evolution gave rise to a script known as "English roundhand." This method of writing came into use in the 17th century, and for all practical purposes it is the same script we use today.

THE HISTORY OF AUTOGRAPH AND MANUSCRIPT COLLECTING

Though we might be stretching the point a bit, one could say that the ancient Sumerians were the first to assemble a "collection" of manuscripts. Engraved on soft clay which was then fired into enduring tablets, the written records of the Sumerians contained information that was vital to the administration of an empire. The tablets were bulky, awkward, and difficult to store, but without question this collection of tablets formed the first "archives" known to civilized man.

The Greek philosopher Aristotle is generally credited with starting the first library: his own, and he used his influence with the ancient kings of Egypt, persuading them to build libraries of their own. Once smitten, the Egyptian kings began to collect with a vengeance; avariciously, they acquired manuscripts of every imaginable description: the end result was the fabulous library of Alexandria, a marvel of the ancient world and the envy of civilized men everywhere.

Naturally, libraries were few and far between, as were collectors. As one might expect, the lure of autograph collecting has little appeal to those who cannot read. The collection of manuscripts and autographs was the prerogative of a select group—limited to monarchs, churchmen, scientists, and philosophers, and so it remained for centuries, until literacy became widespread.

The 1800's saw a vast increase in the number of autograph collectors. Reverend William B. Sprague was the first well-known American collector. Famed for the diversity of his interest, he was originally a tutor in the extended family of George Washington. He began collecting at around the age of 19 or 20 and continued until his death in 1876, at the age of 81.

So collecting autographs and manuscripts for personal and/or historical reasons is not a recent occurrence. However, it is fair to say that it was just during the course of the last ten or fifteen years that collecting has really come into its own. The past decade has seen a sensational increase in the number of collectors, and as a corresponding result prices for material have risen steadily.

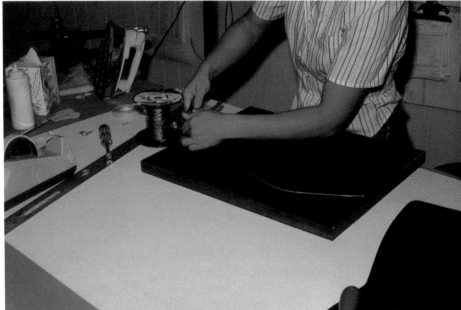

In these three photos, the finishing touches are accomplished: screw eyes are affixed, hanging wire is attached, and bumper pads are placed on the rear of the document display.

An identification tag is placed onto the back of the finished piece.

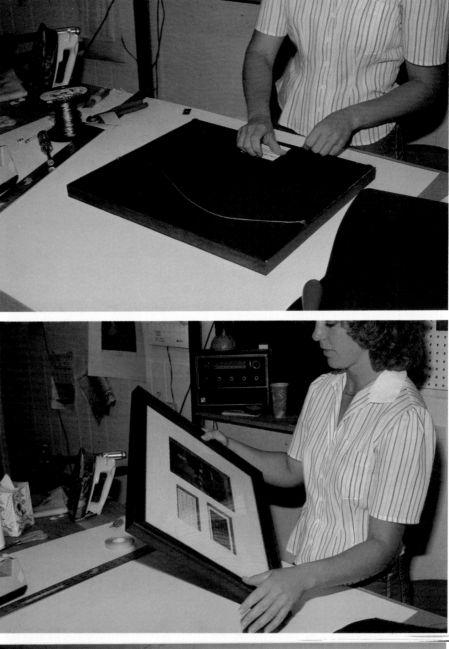

Preserved in an acid-free environment and beautifully matted and framed, the document is ready for hanging. Historical documents are exciting alternatives to more traditional forms of art.

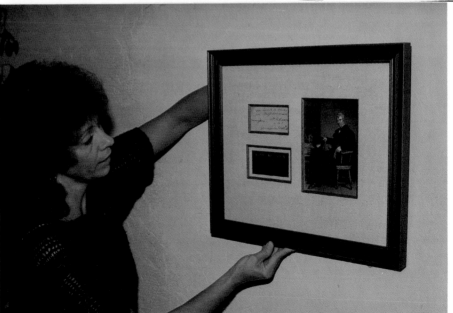

Appendix C
The Signers of the
Declaration of Independence

Over a year had passed since the confrontations in Lexington and Concord; the burdens imposed by England were no longer possible to carry. On June 7, 1776, Richard Henry Lee of Virginia took the floor of the Second Continental Congress and called for a "resolution of independence." The motion carried, and a committee was appointed four days later to prepare the resolution. Benjamin Franklin, John Adams, Robert Livingston, and Thomas Jefferson were to draft the resolution (Jefferson did the actual writing).

The first draft was revised by the committee and sent to Congress where it was revised again. The resolution was adopted on July 2, 1776; the document adopted July 4, 1776 (which we know as the Declaration of Independence) was actually an embellished justification of the July 2nd resolution.

Beginning with John Hancock, 50 men signed the Declaration on August 2, 1776; six others signed at another time. Not all the men involved in helping to draft the document and vote for it signed it. (You might be interested to know that while George Washington signed the Constitution, he did not sign the Declaration of Independence—being in the army at the time, he was unable to do so.)

A number of Signers lived to a ripe old age. Many continued with their political activities, becoming governors, senators, congressmen, and presidents. These men led us through one of the most tumultuous periods in our history, and one must recall the size of the stakes involved. Victory meant vindication of rebellion and an unprecedented opportunity to mold a unique politcal entity. Defeat meant treason; the penalty for treason was death. It was an exciting, if precarious, time to be alive, and the writings of these men contain a rich historical legacy way out of proportion to their relatively small numbers.

As one might expect, the giants, Franklin and Jefferson, are (and always have been) in great demand among collectors. Their autograph material commands high prices—and is not always easy to find. At the other end of the spectrum, Robert Morris is probably the least difficult to acquire. Influential and literate, he was a prolific penman.

To assemble a complete collection of Signers, you will have to gather the autographs of 56 men, a challenging proposition. As a broad generalization, it would be fair to say that most of the Signers are not extremely difficult to collect. There are, however, two notable exceptions, and it might be appropriate to mention them at this point. At the present time, only one letter of each of these men is known to be in existence.

BUTTON GWINNETT

The most elusive of the Signers to collect, Gwinnett was born in England and emigrated to America. He settled in Georgia, becoming a successful planter/merchant. In 1776, he was sent to the Continental Congress as a delegate from Georgia. He was elected as Governor of Georgia in 1777, but died that year—at the age of 42—from wounds inflicted in a duel. Autographs and manuscripts authored by him are extremely rare and in tremendous demand.

THOMAS LYNCH, JR.

Son of a well-known South Carolina statesman of the same name (be careful not to confuse the two), Lynch was elected to the Continental Congress in 1776, at the age of 27. He was forced to resign soon thereafter due to poor health. In 1779, he embarked on a vessel bound for the West Indies in the hope that the climate would cure or improve his illness. He was lost at sea.

TABLE OF SIGNERS OF THE
DECLARATION OF INDEPENDENCE

Name	Delegate From	Name	Delegate From
John Adams	Massachusetts	Thomas Lynch, Jr.	South Carolina
Samuel Adams	Massachusetts	Thomas McKean	Delaware
Josiah Bartlett	New Hampshire	Arthur Middleton	South Carolina
Carter Braxton	Virginia	Lewis Morris	New York
Charles Carroll of Carrollton	Maryland	Robert Morris	Pennsylvania
		John Morton	Pennsylvania
Samuel Chase	Maryland	Thomas Nelson, Jr.	Virginia
Abraham Clark	New Jersey	William Paca	Maryland
George Clymer	Pennsylvania	Robert Treat Paine	Massachusetts
William Ellery	Rhode Island	John Penn	North Carolina
William Floyd	New York	George Read	Delaware
Benjamin Franklin	Pennsylvania	Caesar Rodney	Delaware
Elbridge Gerry	Massachusetts	George Ross	Pennsylvania
Button Gwinnett	Georgia	Benjamin Rush	Pennsylvania
Lyman Hall	Georgia	Edward Rutledge	South Carolina
John Hancock	Massachusetts	Roger Sherman	Connecticut
Benjamin Harrison	Virginia	James Smith	Pennsylvania
John Hart	New Jersey	Richard Stockton	New Jersey
Joseph Hewes	North Carolina	Thomas Stone	Maryland
Thomas Heyward, Jr.	South Carolina	George Taylor	Pennsylvania
William Hooper	North Carolina	Matthew Thornton	New Hampshire
Stephen Hopkins	Rhode Island	George Walton	Georgia
Francis Hopkinson	New Jersey	William Whipple	New Hampshire
Samuel Huntington	Connecticut	William Williams	Connecticut
Thomas Jefferson	Virginia	James Wilson	Pennsylvania
Francis Lightfoot Lee	Virginia	John Witherspoon	New Jersey
Richard Henry Lee	Virginia	Oliver Wolcott	Connecticut
Francis Lewis	New York	George Wythe	Virginia
Philip Livingston	New York		

Appendix D
The American Presidents

Without question, assembling American Presidential autographs is one of the most popular areas of collecting in the United States. This select group of men has captured our attention and imagination like no other. Their decisions have affected the lives of all Americans and, as the country matured, the lives of the balance of the world's population. And there is a bonus involved in this type of collecting: presidential material is never out of vogue.

There are no bounds to the categories of collecting. I have mentioned presidential campaign material; another area is presidential checks. You may also be interested in collecting the memorabilia of vice-presidents or cabinet members and leading officials. You can easily conjure up a score of common denominators that relate the men who have held the position of Chief Executive of the United States. These men share the joint distinction of high office. What other areas for collecting come to mind? Religion, education, diplomacy, relations with their respective parties, presidential wives, personal tastes, habits, thoughts on any given subject from slavery to tariff regulations—the possibilities are endless.

Because of the vast amount of material involved, I would advise you to plan your collection carefully. Here, especially, an overall perspective is essential. Bear in mind that content, while always important, is a crucial factor in determining the value and availability of presidential autographs.

There are many books available that cover the American Presidency in minute detail (one example is *The American Presidents,* David C. Whitney, 1982). While it is not possible to present that vast volume of material here, I have decided to touch upon a few of the presidents whose achievements and personalities have made them exceptional in a group of outstanding men. These are just thumbnail sketches of some of the men who shaped our country's destiny—before, as well as during, their terms as President. If you become involved in collecting presidential autographs, perhaps you will be fortunate enough, as I have, to get a glimpse of the flesh and blood human being behind the smiling facade of the professional politician.

GEORGE WASHINGTON

One of the most admired—and collected—presidents, Washington managed to cram an incredible amount of living into his 67 years. Trained as a surveyor, at age 16 he plied his trade west of the Blue Ridge Mountains in what was then wilderness territory. Six years later he was a colonel fighting the French. In May of 1754, Washington attained his first military victory, but two months later, on July 4, he was forced to surrender to a superior French force. Repatriated soon thereafter, he served an additional four years.

In 1759, he married Martha Custis, and that same year he became a member of the Virginia House of Burgesses, serving until 1774, when he was elected as a delegate to the Continental Congress.

Mainly due to the strong influence of John Adams, Washington took command of the Continental Army on July 3, 1775. This so-called "army" was a rag-tag band of poorly equipped, untrained militia. Washington himself was inexperienced in commanding a large force in major engagements, but he learned quickly. He survived the British, the clique in the Congress who were determined to remove him from his command, and his own shortcomings—going on to serve as President from 1789 to 1797. He well deserved the title "Father of Our Country."

Although there is a tremendous demand for letters and manuscripts penned during the war years and his terms as President, letters predating the war are more readily available. A collection centered around his formative years as a young officer would shed interesting light on his later experiences.

THOMAS JEFFERSON

Political philosopher, scientist, inventor, architect, and a brilliant writer, Jefferson was the epitome of the eternal student, enthralled by every aspect of human endeavor. Always prey to a restless sense of curiosity, Jefferson was one of the most inquisitive and productive men of his era.

Jefferson was only 33 years old when he drafted the Declaration of Independence, and his life spanned another half-century, during which time he served two terms (1801-1809) as third president of the United States.

Jefferson was a diligent letter writer (compilations of his correspondence fill countless volumes), and thousands of his letters still exist. Nearly all of these letters share two attributes: they demonstrate his consistently careless attitude towards punctuation, and the text of his letters is nearly always smaller than his signature. Like those of Washington, his letters are interesting and in great demand.

ANDREW JACKSON

First hero of the American common man, Jackson's script remained consistent with his character. Renowned for his volatile disposition, he was a man who tolerated little foolishness in his friends—or from the Congress. His penmanship was consistent with his political mien—bold, forthright, and without apology. His poor spelling and direct language add more than a little spice to his letters, and his presence would add vitality to any collection.

ABRAHAM LINCOLN

The details of Lincoln's life are so well known to every schoolboy that it seems almost foolish to attempt to profile them here. Frontiersman, lawyer, orator, and consummate politician, Lincoln's life is an inspiration to all human beings who cherish freedom. We can only surmise how enlightened the period of Reconstruction might have been had he survived the assassin's bullet.

Like Washington, Lincoln was a prolific correspondent. His letters ignore the formal niceties of the day and almost always have the appearance of being hastily—even carelessly—written. Of all autographs, his is the most prized. Lincoln's holographic papers are always in demand and usually very expensive.

THEODORE ROOSEVELT

Scion of an old New York family, Roosevelt's fragile health as a youngster gave no hint of the vigorous man who emerged to become Commander of the Rough Riders and the 26th President of the United States. Launching his political career in the New York State Legislature in 1882, Roosevelt served just two short years.

Heartbroken at the deaths of his wife and mother and politically damaged by his loyal support of James G. Blaine's disastrous presidential campaign, he opted for the vast spaces of his ranch in the Dakota Territory. Vitality restored, he returned to New York in 1886 and ran unsuccessfully for mayor. Until the outbreak of the Spanish-American War in 1898, he involved himself in the Republican Party and held various posts as a Member of the Civil Service Commission, Chairman of the New York City Police Board, and Assistant Secretary of the Navy. He became known to the general public for his unimpeachable integrity and outspoken honesty.

But it was the war in Cuba that made Roosevelt a household name. Returning a national hero, the Rough Rider promptly ran for Governor of New York, a race he won by a small margin. His success annoyed the political bosses, and they smugly supported him for Vice-President, seeking to neutralize him politically.

Fate would have it otherwise, and Roosevelt became President of the United States when a bullet fired by Leon Czolgosz, a deluded anarchist, ended President McKinley's life. Roosevelt later won re-election in his own right and oversaw one of the most dramatic and formative periods of American history.

Few people realize that he was awarded the Nobel Peace Prize in 1906 for his success in mediating an end to the Russo-Japanese War. Like Andrew Jackson, Roosevelt expressed himself with vigor. Ever the fighting man, his letters reflect his ire when aroused as well as his intellectual depth. Much Roosevelt material is typewritten, but—to use his own word—would make a "bully" object of collection.

FRANKLIN DELANO ROOSEVELT

Perhaps the most skillful of all American politicians, FDR's four terms of service set a record that can never be equaled. Leading the country from the depths of the Depression through all but the last year of World War II, Roosevelt left his personal stamp on America as few presidents have since the time of Abraham Lincoln. And, unlike her predecessors, his wife, Eleanor, was certainly one of the most vital and respected women of this century.

Like his cousin Theodore, FDR served as a vigorous and capable Assistant Secretary of the Navy before running as Vice-Presidential candidate on the Democratic ticket with the now-forgotten James M. Cox. A year later he was stricken with poliomyletis and left crippled until the end of his life.

Though sick and despondent, with the support of his remarkable wife he regained his strength—and rekindled his interest in politics. By 1928 he was Governor of New York; four years later he was in the White House, having utterly crushed his hapless predecessor, Herbert Hoover.

FDR's first three months in office, known as the "Hundred Days," saw a volume of legislation that changed the structure of the country's economic life and philosophy. His "Fireside Chats" brought him close to the hearts of the Americans beset by economic depression and war.

His letters are noted for their great warmth and charm. Holographic material originating during his terms of office is rare. As previously mentioned, at one time or another Roosevelt used seven different aides who were authorized to sign his name. Several were quite adept, and I recommend that you exercise caution in dealing with Roosevelt autographs—be sure that you verify the hand.

JOHN FITZGERALD KENNEDY

Mention Kennedy's name in any gathering of Americans over thirty, and you will evoke wistful memories. The nation was prosperous and at the pinnacle of economic prosperity and international prestige, and Kennedy (at 43, the youngest president to be elected) fit the country's mood. Vigorous, charming, and possessed of a wit that delighted the nation, Kennedy gathered around him men of talent and intellect. The brilliance of his political speeches inspired not only Americans, but freedom-loving peoples all over the world.

Kennedy's brief term of office took place during an era of confrontation: the Bay of Pigs fiasco, the Cuban Missile Crisis, the Berlin Wall, pressure in Viet Nam, the Civil Rights issue in this country. But the Peace Corps, the Space Program, medical care for the aged, and federal aid to economically beleaguered areas were just some of the programs that flourished under his direction (although many were completed by his successor, Lyndon Baines Johnson). Some efforts, like the civil rights legislation, Medicare, the Peace Corps, and the Space Program enriched and bettered the lives of millions of Americans; other entanglements, such as our involvement in Viet Nam, bore bitter fruit.

Aside from the fact that Kennedy's term of office represented a key point in American history, no one can deny that he made an indelible impression on the hearts of millions of Americans. Next to Lincoln's, Kennedy's autograph material is prized above all other presidents; and few of his letters are offered for sale. Verification of his handwriting is best left to experts because his script was remarkably inconsistent—and he did make extensive use of the Autopen.

TABLE OF THE PRESIDENTS
OF THE UNITED STATES

Name	Born	Died	Presidential Term	Wife
George Washington	02/22/1732	12/14/1799	04/30/1789-03/03/1797	Martha (Dandridge) Custis
John Adams	10/30/1735	07/04/1826	03/04/1797-03/03/1801	Abigail Smith
Thomas Jefferson	04/13/1743	07/04/1826	03/04/1801-03/03/1809	Martha (Wayles) Skelton
James Madison	03/16/1751	06/28/1836	03/04/1809-03/03/1817	Dorothea "Dolly" (Payne) Todd
James Monroe	04/28/1758	07/04/1831	03/04/1817-03/03/1825	Elizabeth Kortright
John Q. Adams	07/11/1767	02/23/1848	03/04/1825-03/03/1829	Louisa Catherine Johnson
Andrew Jackson	03/15/1767	06/08/1845	03/04/1829-03/03/1837	Rachel (Donelson) Robards
Martin Van Buren	12/05/1782	07/24/1862	03/04/1837-03/03/1841	Hannah Hoe
William H. Harrison	02/09/1773	04/04/1841	03/04/1841-04/04/1841	Anna Symmes
John Tyler	03/29/1790	01/18/1862	04/06/1841-03/03/1845	Letitia Christian (d. 1842); Julia Gardiner
James K. Polk	11/02/1795	06/15/1849	03/04/1845-03/03/1849	Sara Childress
(David R. Atchison)	08/11/1807	01/26/1886	03/04/1849	
Zachary Taylor	11/24/1784	07/09/1850	03/05/1849-07/09/1850	Margaret Smith
Millard Fillmore	01/07/1800	03/08/1874	07/10/1850-03/03/1853	Abigail Powers
Franklin Pierce	11/23/1804	10/08/1869	03/04/1853-03/03/1857	Jane Means Appleton
James Buchanan	04/23/1791	06/01/1868	03/04/1857-03/03/1861	
Abraham Lincoln	02/12/1809	04/15/1865	03/04/1861-04/15/1865	Mary Todd
Andrew Johnson	12/29/1808	07/31/1875	04/15/1865-03/03/1869	Eliza McCardle
Ulysses S. Grant	04/27/1822	07/23/1885	03/04/1869-03/03/1877	Julia Dent
Rutherford B. Hayes	10/04/1822	01/17/1893	03/04/1877-03/03/1881	Lucy Ware Webb
James Garfield	11/19/1831	09/19/1881	03/04/1881-09/19/1881	Lucretia Rudolph
Chester Arthur	10/05/1829	11/18/1886	09/20/1881-03/03/1885	Ellen Lewis Herndon
Grover Cleveland	03/18/1837	06/24/1908	03/04/1885-03/03/1889	Frances Folsom
Benjamin Harrison	08/20/1833	03/13/1901	03/04/1889-03/03/1893	Caroline Lavinia Scott
Grover Cleveland	03/18/1837	06/24/1908	03/04/1893-03/03/1897	Frances Folsom
William McKinley	01/29/1843	09/14/1901	03/04/1897-09/14/1901	Ida Saxton
Theodore Roosevelt	10/27/1858	01/06/1919	09/14/1901-03/03/1909	Edith Kermit Carow
William H. Taft	09/15/1857	03/08/1930	03/04/1909-03/03/1913	Helen Herron
Woodrow Wilson	12/28/1856	02/03/1924	03/04/1913-03/03/1921	Ellen Louise Axson (d. 1914); Edith (Bolling) Galt
Warren G. Harding	11/02/1865	08/02/1923	03/04/1921-08/02/1923	Florence (Kling) De Wolfe
Calvin Coolidge	07/04/1872	01/05/1933	08/03/1923-03/03/1929	Grace Anna Goodhue
Herbert Hoover	08/10/1874	10/20/1964	03/04/1929-03/03/1933	Lou Henry
Franklin Roosevelt	01/30/1882	04/12/1945	03/04/1933-04/12/1945	Anna Eleanor Roosevelt
Harry Truman	05/08/1884	12/26/1972	04/13/1945-01/20/1953	Elizabeth "Bess" Wallace
Dwight Eisenhower	10/14/1890	03/28/1969	01/20/1953-01/20/1961	Mamie Geneva Doud
John F. Kennedy	05/29/1917	11/22/1963	01/20/1961-11/22/1963	Jacqueline Lee Bouvier
Lyndon B. Johnson	08/27/1908	01/22/1973	11/22/1963-01/20/1969	Claudia Alta "Lady Bird" Taylor
Richard Nixon	01/09/1913		01/20/1969-08/09/1974	Thelma Catherine Patricia "Pat" Ryan
Gerald Ford	07/14/1913		08/09/1974-01/20/1977	Elizabeth "Betty" (Bloomer) Warren
Jimmy Carter	10/01/1924		01/20/1977-01/20/1981	Rosalynn Smith
Ronald Reagan	02/06/1911		01/20/1981-	Nancy Davis

Glossary

AUTOGRAPH: can mean a simple signature, but among collectors, usually signifies a piece of writing entirely in the author's hand. (See also HOLOGRAPH)

AUTOGRAPH LETTER: a hand-written, unsigned letter.

BID: the amount of money offered for material at auction sales.

BROADSIDE: a folio sheet, unfolded, with printing on one side only. Used in colonial times to convey information.

CONTEMPORARY COPY: a copy made about the same time as the original. Before the advent of carbon paper and copy machines, there was no way to make a simultaneous copy.

CORRESPONDENCE: letters, postcards, memoranda, notes, telegrams, or any other forms of addressed communications, sent and received.

DAMP-STAINED: damage to an autograph or manuscript (usually not too severe) by moisture.

DE-ACIDIFICATION: the process by which the corrosive action of ink and paper is arrested.

DOCKET: a filing notation made on the back side of a document.

DOCUMENT: usually taken to mean a form, completed by hand, whose intended purpose was to transmit or preserve information.

ENCAPSULATION: a simple process by which an autograph is preserved by encasing it in a Mylar sheath.

ENDORSEMENT: found on the reverse side of checks, signature that acknowledges receipt of same; may also include comments or notations.

FACSIMILES: exact copies of original pieces.

FAIR COPY: a copy created to be "suitable for framing" such as a few stanzas of a poem written out by the author and signed by him.

FOLIO: a large sheet of paper on which several or many pages of a book were printed. The sheet was then folded and cut to create individual pages. (See also SIZES)

FOXING: spotting created on an autograph as a result of mold or mildew.

FRANKING: The "frank" is a privilege granted to certain individuals by their governments and allows them to send letters and other items through the mails at no cost—by simply writing their signatures in place of a stamp.

HOLOGRAPH: a piece of writing entirely in the author's hand and signed by him.

HOLOGRAPHIC LETTER: a letter written entirely in the author's hand and signed by him.

INLAYING: matting a document by gluing its edges to a cut piece of matboard.

LAMINATION: a preservation process whereby the document is heat-sealed between sheets of cellulose acetate. This process obscures the autograph somewhat and is not favored by collectors.

LETTERPRESS: a manual press which produced copies by pressing a blank piece of paper onto a wet original.

LOT: in an auction sale, a group of material sold at one time.

MONOGRAM: a form of signature; letters arranged in a square, connected by diagonal, horizontal, or vertical lines. Usually drawn by a scribe, some portion was always added personally by the person represented.

OCTAVO (abbreviated "8vo"): a sheet from a folded folio, measuring approximately 6″ × 9″. (See also SIZES)

PARAPH: an addition to a signature in the form of a flourish or swirl below or behind the signature; originally intended to prevent forgery.

PICTOGRAM: a pictorial design adopted and used as a signature.

PROVENANCE: the chain of title or ownership of a document.

QUARTO (abbreviated "4to"): a sheet from a folded folio, measuring approximately 9″ × 12″—although the size can vary an inch (plus or minus) on both dimensions. (See also SIZES)

RECTO: the front side of a piece of writing.

SIGNATURE: the name of a person written in his own hand and in the fashion in which he habitually writes it; also called an autograph.

SIGNUM: a sign used in place of a signature, originally often in the shape of a cross.

SILKING: a preservation process in which the autograph is covered with silk gauze, applied with archival quality paste. This somewhat obscures the autograph, and silking must be replaced every fifteen years.

SIZES: portions of a folded folio sheet. Include: QUARTO (4to), 9″ × 12″; OCTAVO (8vo), 6″ × 9″; TWELVEMO (12mo) or SMALL OCTAVO, 5″ × 7″; SIXTEENMO, 4″ × 7″.

SPOTTED: the autograph has been marred by large stains.

STRENGTHENED ALONG FOLDS: a tissue has been pasted along a fold to strengthen it.

TRANSCRIPT: a copy of an autograph or manuscript made by someone other than the author of the original.

TYPESCRIPT: Typed letter or document exactly as or similar to the original but accomplished after the fact, signed by the same person(s) who signed the original. Occasionally a related party is authorized to sign, *i.e.,* Grand Admiral Karl Doenitz did not actually sign the original German Surrender of World War II but ordered the original to be signed under his authority. However, most typescripts of the German Surrender are signed by Doenitz.

VERSO: the reverse side of a piece of writing.

WATERSTAINED: the autograph or manuscript has been damaged by immersion.

WORN ALONG FOLDS: an autograph has experienced extensive wear along its folded portions.

Index

This index is divided into two parts: text and illustrations.

General Index

Illustrations Index

PRESIDENTS OF

George Washington   1789-1797

John Adams   1797-1801

James K. Polk   1845-1849

Thomas Jefferson   1801-1809

Zachary Taylor   1849-1850

James Madison   1809-1817

Millard Fillmore   1850-1853

James Monroe   1817-1825

Franklin Pierce   1853-1857

John Quincy Adams   1825-1829

James Buchanan   1857-1861

Andrew Jackson   1829-1837

Abraham Lincoln   1861-1865

Martin Van Buren   1837-1841

Andrew Johnson   1865-1869

William Henry Harrison   Mar.-April 1841

Ulysses S. Grant   1869-1877

John Tyler   1841-1845

Rutherford B. Hayes   1877-1881